NEWTOWN

The Story of a School

NEWTOWN

The Story of a School

The First Hundred Years

ANDY MILROY

ACKNOWLEDGEMENTS

First, I would like to thank my wife for her encouragement and proof reading – without it, this book would still be languishing on my computer.

I intended to publish this book in 2000 to celebrate the centenary. Regrettably, for various reasons this did not happen, and so I am very pleased that the project has now finally come to fruition.

This book is a team effort. Without the contributions from former pupils and teachers, it would not exist. I am indebted to all who have made this possible, including articles from pupils taken from the *Newtown Magazine* from the 1960s.

Maureen Duffy was contacted, and her publisher Virago Press agreed to the inclusion of the extract from her book *That's How It Was* about the 11-plus at Newtown.

First Published in Great Britain in 2017 by DB Publishing,
an imprint of JMD Media Ltd

ISBN 9781780915685

Printed and bound in the UK

CONTENTS

FOREWORD

Newtown School, Trowbridge and its various earlier elements has been a major pillar of Trowbridge life for well over a century. Its former pupils make up a sizeable part of the community, especially of those over sixty; when they went to school there were just two junior schools in the town.

This book is intended to give a brief history of the school and its buildings, but at its core are the accounts by former pupils and teachers of their experiences of the schools.

The school emerged from the non-conformist tradition in the town, which was the driving force behind its industry and commerce. The fascinating history of the school in the 20th century continues to reflect the development of the town, and its growing diversity as different nationalities were drawn to work in the industries of Trowbridge.

In many ways the school became a microcosm of the town. It reflected both changes in education legislation, and the changes in numbers echoed the geographic expansion to the south of the town centre and west of the railway line, less restricted than to the north, which meant that Parochial School, the only other early school, was to be less affected by the growth in pupil numbers.

The viewpoints of the pupils and teachers, through their accounts, reflect these changes and show the impact of the school on individuals, and the section on former pupils shows how the school in turn was to influence the town.

A BRIEF HISTORY OF THE SCHOOLS IN NEWTOWN

The Newtown building is described in *The Buildings of England – Wiltshire* by Nikolaus Pevsner, 1963, as 'Extremely pretty … and symmetrical, in a domestic neo-Baroque'.[1]

An early H.M.I. commented 'the most beautiful and up-to-date school in the West of England'. The *Victoria County History Vol. VII* states: 'The school was considered both in the design of its buildings and the methods of its teaching to be in the forefront of educational progress'.

The Newtown Area

Right up until the 1970s and later, Newtown was perceived as a distinct community, detached from the town of Trowbridge. Called Newtown because it was built outside the Parish of Trowbridge, the river and the railway line acted as a barrier between the Newtown community and the town. A drawing from sometime after 1848 shows Trowbridge as a distant industrial vista, with sheep grazing in the foreground and the railway cutting and steam locomotive behind.

Newtown was a self-contained area with a variety of small shops. A trip to the town was only needed for the bigger purchases. Everyday groceries could be purchased; Newtown could boast several small grocers, a newsagent/sweetshop, a greengrocer, a branch of the Co-op, a butcher, a dress shop and others. Sleightholms, the garage, was on the corner, at the top of Newtown (the site now long-developed as flats) where they catered as much for the bicycle as

---

1   The school appears in the Department of the Environment's *List of Buildings of Special Architectural or Historic Interest*. It is a Grade II listed building. The listing describes it as: '1900 by Silcox [sic] and Ray [sic] of Bath. Queen Anne Revival. Red brick with stone dressings. The street front has a recessed central gable with lower flanking projecting pavilions having semicircular stone porch hoods with Ionic columns and semi-circular fanlights [with glazing bars]. The pavilions have flanking windows with glazing bar sashes and moulded architraves; balastrade over cornice. Main gable has modillion verge cornice and cornice to ground floor through which the round head of the main Venetian window breaks [this part with Gibbs surround]. The Venetian window has Doric columns. Below is a large cartouche inscribed "This stone was laid by Sir Roger Brown April 28th 1900". Pretty pepperpot belfry in centre of tiled roof.' ST 8557 6/326

the car. In the adjoining streets could be found wool shops, another branch of the Co-op, a baker, more butchers and grocers, etc.

With a public house actually in Newtown and another on the corner, the Wesley Road Chapel and Holy Trinity Church close by, virtually every need was served. There was little necessity to venture into 'town' unless you required clothes or the market (Trowbridge still boasted a cattle market at that time), or something else not available in Newtown itself.

The area bounded by Frome Road and Wingfield Road, extending south-west from Newtown, was originally common field with north–south strips of land laid out in the medieval pattern. This land was then eventually enclosed with hedges and subsequently sold off. The later street plan of the area appears to preserve this ancient field pattern.

In 1660, John Stallard was reported for building a dwelling on the Waste close to what is now the corner of Stallard Street and Newtown. The Waste was literally the uncultivated road verge, on the edge of the common land. The custom at that time was that if a squatter built his dwelling, complete with a roof, and had a fire burning inside within a day, he was entitled to stay there. This custom had no basis in law, but was generally accepted at this time by both the poor and those in authority. His seems to have been the first house in the Newtown area, and marks the beginning of the 'new town'. The area had been known for centuries as Pilewell, but soon became known as Newtown.

Other small cottages were soon built close by; the former shop of A. Semeraro, the shoe repairer, gives some idea of what they might have been like. The rest of these were demolished in about 1939 as part of a slum clearance. In 1790, the row of terraced three-storey weavers' cottages was built, in which the top storey was clearly a workshop, frequently having larger windows than the lower floors. These workshops were originally used by weavers, who used narrow looms to make a kind of cloth called cassimeres.

The western side of Newtown was eventually completed with the construction of Pilewell Terrace in the 1820s [the first built in 1823], with the Wesley Road Chapel being built in 1872. Amidst the row of the terrace of weavers' cottages, some bottom storeys were turned into shops, and a public house, the Rising Sun, was opened. The eastern side of Newtown was built up between 1892 and 1904 by several small local building firms. A space was left in the middle of this development for the one missing amenity in this community – a school.

Education in Trowbridge

At the beginning of the 19th century there were several private schools, and dame schools in the town, but the major centre of education in Trowbridge was the Free School in St James' Churchyard. This was run by the Church of England but took the boys of non-conformist families. At that time, Trowbridge was an area very strong in non-conformist views, and many people felt that these children were being exposed to C of E doctrine.

In 1808, what was to become the British and Foreign School Society was formed in London to provide non-sectarian religious education for the children of England.

A branch of the society met in Trowbridge in 1832, to consider building a British School. The local clothiers gave money towards the building of the British School, which was erected in 1832 in Frog Lane or British Row – so non-sectarian education was provided at one end of the town, but not the other. The new school was a rival to the National Church of England School which was in St James' Churchyard. The former Parochial School building, opposite the churchyard, was not built until 1846.

By the 1890s, the Newtown area had developed so rapidly that it was felt necessary to have a non-sectarian school at that end of the town. The Holy Trinity Schools at Stallard Street and Park Street were there, but non-conformists thought that members of the Church of England were favoured. There was a clause in the school rules called the Conscience Clause, which said no doctrine should be taught to non-conformist children against the wishes of their parents. This clause, however, was not always kept. It was the rule that religious instruction should always be the first or last lesson of the day, to enable parents to withdraw their children.

There were many non-conformist places of worship in Trowbridge at this time – at the Conigre and Manvers Street, and the Emmanuel, Zion, Bethesda and Tabernacle chapels and churches. There were consequently many moneyed non-conformists among the clothiers and industrialists in Trowbridge. Many of these were members of the East Somerset and Wiltshire Congregational Union. In 1897, William J. Mann was the president of the union, George N. Haden was a former treasurer and Sir W. Roger Brown had been the auditor for many years. This group were to be major supporters of the idea of a new non-denominational school in the town.

In 1897, the desirability of a new school in the Newtown area came before the committee of the Old British Schools, and a resolution was passed that a day school should be started there.

Following that decision, negotiations were opened with the Rev. W.T. Gill and the trustees of the Wesley Road Wesleyan Church for the use of their Sunday school room for the new school as an interim measure. They gave their 'hearty co-operation' and the Education Department agreed, on condition that a 'large and commodious school' was erected.

In August 1898, the Wesley Road Sunday School was to be occupied as 'a day school for elementary education'. A sum of £140 was spent in improving the sanitary and other arrangements. Thus, the school was able to start immediately.

The committee next decided to launch an appeal for the erection of a British School in Newtown. The appeal stated: 'The term British expresses in a word the broad character of the education to be given. The religious basis of the British School system is what is termed undenominational – there is absolutely no teaching of a sectarian character.'

The funding for the proposed new school building was to come from the wealthy, leading non-conformists. The Rev. Harry Sanders, Secretary of the Committee, later gave an account of how much of the funding for the new school was raised.

The site for the new school was given by Sir W. Roger Brown, one of the leading woollen manufacturers in the town. Harry Sanders wrote:

This [I think] he meant to be his share of the work. I remember calling upon him soon after the gift of the site, and asking him to suggest to me how the money could be raised. He promptly named certain people who would give me large sums. I expressed my doubts. Then he suggested that the working men of the town would give a large sum towards it. I answered that wages were not good enough to lead us to expect much from the working people. He doubted this. I soon convinced him that weavers could not do it. Sir Roger then promised me £500 towards the new building, saying he thought five others could be found in the town to do the same. Again, I expressed my doubts. Mr W.J. Mann was present at the time, and there and then promised another £500.

The Haden family was to give £620, whilst £200 came from the late John Stancomb and £250 from the Usher family.

When this group of non-conformist worthies looked around for an architect for the proposed school, it is perhaps not surprising that they chose Thomas Ball Silcock. Silcock was a well-established architect, and was also the president of the East Somerset and Wiltshire Congregational Union in 1898, the year following William Mann's term of office. The non-conformists in this period were a very close-knit group, and worked together very closely.

The Tabernacle Church minutes of May 1899 recorded:

The scheme to provide a Newtown British School is making progress. More than £1600 has been most generously promised to the building fund by certain members of the Tabernacle ... The Trinity Parish contains more than 5000 souls, so it is imperative that we should provide therefore for the education of our children. If we neglect to do so the young people of many of our Nonconformist homes will drift steadily from the faith of their fathers.

The Beginning

The new school was opened in its temporary premises at 10 a.m. on 29 August 1898. One hundred and eighty children were registered on that first day. This initial enthusiasm may have fallen away somewhat, for the official figures show that eventually there were 46 boys and 45 girls in the mixed classes, and 32 boys and 27 girls in the infants. The head of the school was Mr William Hodgson, with Miss Ada Chandler in charge of the infants. Mr Hodgson was a stocky man of medium height, and clean shaven.

The temporary classrooms were rather cramped and stuffy. 'Ventilation in both rooms is very faulty – when weather is warm the room becomes almost unbearable,' commented Mr Hodgson in the school logbook.

However, this did not seem to affect the brains of the children too much. In April 1899, an HM Inspector of Schools, a Mr Curry, visited the school. Examining a class in mental arithmetic, he asked, 'Supposing my hat cost 3s. 6d., what would be the value of half of it?'

Several hands were immediately held up. Pointing at a girl named Hulbert, he said: 'Now, my child, what do you say?'

The answer was startling and unexpected. 'Nothing,' she said. 'If your hat were cut in two it would be no good.'

Mr Curry was so pleased with the cuteness of the little girl that he gave a monetary reward.

The staff and children had the new school to look forward to, and the head later commented, 'The plans of our new schools, together with the timetable, are to be exhibited at the forthcoming "Paris Exhibition" as typical of a Modern British School.'

In January 1900, work was begun in preparing the Newtown site, and the house, that had previously been built on the site, was pulled down.

The Laying of the Foundation Stone: 5 May 1900

The day for the big open-air ceremony of laying the foundation stone for the new school was viewed with some misgiving, following the 'dull, leaden sky' of the day before, but on the Saturday there was beautiful summer-like weather.

It had been arranged that a procession of school children, together with the committee and friends, should march from the Town Hall to the site of the new building. The children were marshalled in Prospect Place then marched in procession to the Town Hall, where they were joined by the committee.

Headed by the Volunteer Band playing 'Listen to the Band', the procession then marched up Fore Street, the Parade and Stallard Street to the new school site. The procession was watched by large crowds of people, the majority of whom joined in the procession at the rear.

About a dozen wagons had been hired to carry the infant children, and these had been decorated with bunting and evergreens. Altogether 996 children took part in the procession, from the British boys and British girls schools, from Conigre Infant school, from Margaret Stancomb Memorial school (as it was then called), and from Newtown British School. They wore flowers, rosettes and carried miniature Union Jacks.

The new school was obviously still a building site, but great efforts had been made to decorate the site, including streamers from the scaffolding and numerous flags, chiefly Union Jacks and the Stars and Stripes hung from the main building.

A large platform had been erected in front of the memorial stone, which had been draped with the flag of the Empire. The children were lined up within the walls of the structure, and soon after Sir Roger Brown drove up and was greeted by the committee.

The ceremony began with the hymn 'Brightly gleams our banner', the music for which had been composed by Sir Arthur Sullivan, of Gilbert and Sullivan fame. The singing was led by the band, and the children and assembled dignitaries. The vast crowd, which extended some distance along the road, also joined in.

Following this, a passage from the Bible was read, and a prayer said, before another hymn, 'Immortal love, for ever full', was sung.

Mr William Nelson Haden, who presided over the ceremony, stated that the school would be 'thoroughly up to all the modern requirements of an elementary school'. The completed plans had been selected from among a number of others to be sent to the Education Department of the Paris Exhibition, to show what a modern English elementary school was and should be.

Mr Charles Ingram Haden, treasurer of the committee, said that in total £2,377 had been raised, but it was estimated that the school and other expenses would come to £5,600.

The Rev. W.T. Gill, chairman of the committee, said that some would remember when Trowbridge was in the forefront of the West of England cloth industry. That did not depend so much on the machinery in the mills, but upon the talents of the men who handled the machines. The committee hoped the boys and girls would be 'well equipped for the various duties which would come before them'.

After the architect, Thomas Ball Silcock, had described the new building to the assembled crowds, Sir Roger Brown was presented with a carnation buttonhole by Florence Rogers, the senior scholar of Newtown School. Then

Willie Whitman, the eldest boy at the school, presented Sir Roger with a silver trowel with ivory handle. In accepting the gift, Sir Roger said, 'I thank you very much and I hope as I am going to lay the stone with this trowel it will be laid level and perfectly regular, so through life your conduct will be the same.'

The stone was then laid. Sir Roger carefully surveyed the level, and after several sound taps, declared the stone 'well and truly laid'. This announcement was followed by loud cheers. The inscription on the stone read 'This stone was laid by Sir Roger Brown, April 28th 1900'.

In his speech, Sir Roger Brown made clear the aims in building the new school: 'that the children of this country should be placed in such a position that they should not be handicapped by those with whom they competed. As to citizenship … If there was anything better more than another that made a good citizen it was to know how he was to use his political power; and [Sir Roger] did not see how one could do so unless he was properly taught in his youth.' The assembled crowd were invited to place contributions to the cost of building the school upon the foundation stone. £123 13s. 8½d. was collected, to which Sir Roger Brown added a further £50.

The ceremony closed with the National Anthem, and afterwards the children marched back to the Town Hall where they were provided with tea, paid for by Sir Roger Brown.

During the ceremony the architect was much praised: 'The building was a great credit to the architect.'

The builder of the school, Jacob Long of the firm of Jacob Long & Sons of Bath, was also present at the ceremony.

By the time the new school was finished, there were 200 children being taught in the Wesley Road Sunday School premises, and there was a waiting list of 150. The premises were greatly overcrowded, only 120 should have been taught in the Wesley Road building. This was proof of the necessity for a school in Newtown.

The Opening of the School: 27 March 1901

William Hodgson was pleased to be leaving the cramped, poorly ventilated temporary premises. He wrote in the school logbook, on hearing that the school would finally be moving into the new buildings:

A few more lessons here,
Where oxygen is rare
And we shall reach an ampler place
And breathe a purer air

The opening ceremony was on Wednesday, 27 March 1901. The seating capacity of the large hall was taken to its utmost limits. On a temporarily erected platform was Mr William J. Mann, to whom had been delegated the duty of declaring the school open. He had been one of the major contributors to the building of the school. He was supported by MP Charles Morley, Chairman of the National Education Association, Rev. J. Laverack, Rev. A.J. Pearse, Charles Haden and the Rev. Harry Sanders, Minister of Bethesda. Gertrude Grist presented a buttonhole to Mr Morley.

Proceedings at the opening ceremony commenced with the singing of the hymn 'Forward be our watchword', followed later by 'Onward Christian Soldiers'.

(In the *Wiltshire Times* column 'March of Times letters', an old Trowbridgian, Tom Mattocks, remembered that at the age of five and a pupil at Margaret Stancomb School, the children had been invited to attend. The infants from Margaret Stancomb had been taken to Newtown in a lorry drawn by a steam engine roller. The children had been taught to sing 'Onward Christian Soldiers' for the opening.)

Sir Roger Brown was unable to attend the actual opening due to illness, but Mr Mann, the chairman, spoke of the generosity of the former in providing the site and the liberal way in which the Wesleyan Friends had enabled them in their move from the Sunday school hall. The chairman said he hoped the school would long be an emblem of religious equality which would prevail for generations among the people of Trowbridge.

There was a letter of apology from the vicar of Holy Trinity, regretting his non-attendance due to unavoidable circumstances. This was proof of the good feeling between the two schools. Harry Sanders stated clearly that they were not trying to ruin Holy Trinity School. They were simply trying to put within reach of parents who so desired non-sectarian education for their children.

Mr Charles Haden, the committee's treasurer, said that without Mr Mann's work the school would not have been built. They were indebted to him, they were indebted to the other supporters of the school, and, he joked, they were also indebted to the bank to the tune of £1,957.

The cost of the school, including heating and ventilating, architect's fees, interest to the bank, furnishings and all fees, was £6,400. These figures did not include the site, which had been so generously given by Sir Roger Brown. Parents and scholars contributed to the funds as some money was still owing, such contributions represented a great sacrifice for working people.

The view was that the school had been well planned. A school with a central hall of that type was one which would give the headmaster an immense advantage, enabling him to have clear 'observation of each classroom', whilst the side rooms were so nicely lighted by large windows and so conveniently arranged to satisfy any requirements of the school in future.

Mr A. Bourne, Secretary of the British and Foreign School Society, informed the audience that the plans of the Newtown British Schools building had been exhibited first at the Educational Exhibition in London, and subsequently formed part of a collection sent to the Paris Exhibition of 1900. There the collection had been awarded a diploma and the Grand Prix. He would have liked to have shown them the gold medal which represented that prize, but they had been told by the commissionaires that if they wanted the medal they would have to pay for it, and it required 720 francs to purchase it!

The opening ended with the singing of the National Anthem, and then people were invited to walk around the building. A large number afterwards spent some time in an inspection of the building.

The *Wiltshire Times* report on the opening stated that:

The building, which is of the central hall type of elementary school, is a handsome and imposing structure which will add considerably to the attractiveness and dignity of the neighbourhood, solidly constructed of brick with Bath stone facings, it may safely be predicted that it will last for many years, and play an important part in teaching the young of Trowbridge, for many generations. There are two front entrances, one for the boys and the other for the girls.

The larger hall is 67ft by 35ft., and this will be used mainly for standards six and seven. On either side of the hall are two classrooms. The internal structural arrangements are such that from the central hall the principal can command observation of each classroom, while the children in the various rooms will not be exposed to the view of each other. By this scheme where there is a class of, say, sixty, the committee hope to put in charge an assistant teacher, master or mistress, with a pupil and thus get the maximum amount of work at a minimum expense.

From a health point of view, to say nothing of comfort, the arrangements have been elaborately carried out. The cost of ventilating alone will account for a bill of £300. This part of the work has been carried out in most modern style. In the large hall there are five ventilators, while one main shaft leads from all parts of the school into a turret. The heating will be by means of hot water, and for this purpose five large radiators have been placed in the central hall and one in each class-room. Special heating arrangements have been made for both cloak rooms. In addition to a radiator hot water pipes have been fitted in each, so that when heated the rooms will be from ten to twenty degrees warmer than the teaching rooms. Here again this idea has been prompted by a desire for the welfare of the learners. Children who on their way to school have been caught in the rain will thus he enabled to have their coats and wraps dried during school hours. [This heating system was installed, of course, by G.N. Haden & Sons.]

A further advantage, although a somewhat minor one, but still illustrative of the up-to-dateness of the methods adopted, is that each peg is numbered and every scholar will have a prescriptive right to a peg. All the rooms have wood block floors so that the teachers and taught will be troubled with none of the disadvantages which arise from an ordinary board floor, and are alike unpleasant and unhealthy. During military and other physical exercises it will be a great boon to be free from clouds of dust while the absence of vibration will prove an additional benefit. The total number of scholars the school will provide for will be about 420, and on the testimony of His Majesty's Inspector the school is the best of that kind in the West of England.

(The original plans of the building in the Wiltshire and Swindon Records Office show a semi-circular step outside each of the main doors leading out into Newtown. This step is also shown in the drawing of the school reproduced in *The Building News* of 14 June 1901, but as far as I can tell, these steps were never built. The actual drawing, according to that publication, was 'now at the Royal Academy'.)

The First Morning

On 1 April 1901, the first morning of the Newtown British School in its new building, Harry Sanders, who had been instrumental in bringing the school into being, commented in the school logbook: 'The look of complete satisfaction is upon Teachers and scholars as they work under the spacious conditions of the new school. It is bound to increase both the standard of efficiency and health of all concerned.'

The *Wiltshire Times* had reported details of the furnishings of the new school on its opening:

The course of instruction which will be followed in the school will have a great bearing on the commercial side of life and the necessary teaching apparatus is of the most modern kind

Besides a number of desks which will be brought from the present place of instruction, fifty of a greatly improved pattern have been purchased. These desks have several advantages over those of the old style and will prevent any unnecessary thumbing of books while the seat can be turned up and so give the scholar plenty of room for physical exercises without leaving the desks.

Elementary science will play an important part in the general instruction. Object lessons will be given in the various standards on metals and minerals, natural products, and textiles. The children will also have the advantage of studying from contour, or relief-model maps, and to be able to realise the heights of hills and mountains from these maps must assist in no small degree in a scholar's geographical learning, while a further aid in this respect, will be found in some new illustrated geographical readers. For the higher standards a new feature will be introduced in the shape of artistic studies, and this should prove of no small benefit to the elder scholars. The acquisition of a revolving top board with numerous figures – a simple yet clever device – gives a variety of civil service sums and no matter what figures the teacher might present to the pupils to be worked out, the answer is always at hand. Even in the commonest requirements of a schoolroom every article which has been within recent years improved has been procured, and nothing to prevent a good sound education, besides looking after the welfare and comfort of the children, has been over-looked.

However, the fundraising had fallen short of what had been needed to realise the original design of the school in full. The infants' classes at the back of the school had to wait another five years until they were finally built. In the meantime, under their head, Miss Margaret Hartley, the infants continued to work in temporary classrooms in Wesley Road. The new classrooms were finally opened in early May 1905. A new infant toilet block was also added alongside the girls toilets at the same time.

Despite the new surroundings, in the days before modern drugs, particularly penicillin, health was often a major problem in schools. Later that month the infant school was forced to close by an epidemic of measles, and in 1909 deaths among the young scholars were reported from diphtheria. In the adjoining mixed school, too, there were similar problems. In October 1918, it was closed by order of the School Medical Officer because influenza was very rife in the school. It was to stay closed for nearly a month before eventually reopening with 100 children absent.

Meanwhile, in 1909 the Newtown schools had changed their status, having been taken over by the Education Committee. (The buildings themselves had been transferred in 1904.) They now became known as Newtown Council Schools. All the council schools in Trowbridge had the same board of managers, and William Mann was elected chairman. He was to remain as chairman until 1934.

Newtown had soon earned the reputation for being an excellent centre of learning. It was an all-age school, providing education from the children's entry into schooling until they left at 14. As early as April 1901, the head of Trinity Boys School recorded: 'In consequence of the opening of the new British school near our school, several boys have left the school for that school.'

Numbers continued to grow in the Newtown schools. By July 1913, the Director of Education had written to the managers of the school that average attendance had exceeded the recognised accommodation, and Mr Hodgson was informed that no more children must be admitted until the average attendance was reduced to a proper limit. In January 1915, the managers' attention was drawn to the fact that the Newtown Infants School was in breach of the regulations of the Board of Education in allowing one teacher to take a class comprising more than sixty scholars.

However, despite these restrictions, by 1919 the number of children in the schools was such that the hall was used to teach two classes with a screen between them. Newtown's popularity became a considerable problem. By the mid-1920s, there were three classes being taught in the undivided hall.

For the infant classes, taught in the three classrooms at the back of the school, one on the left wing of the mixed department and two on the right wing, there were even greater pressures. Each of those classrooms had close to fifty pupils in them. It was hardly surprising that the stress caused Miss Hartley to become ill.

In addition, the playground accommodation was hardly suitable, being regarded as slippery and potentially dangerous.[2] Plans were considered to level the gradient, and build steps up to the Newtown building. However, this idea was disregarded in favour of covering the gradient with 'crude tar and gravel' in July 1915. However, the loose gravel caused accidents and had to be scraped off. Despite this, the headmaster received complaints that 'the boys were constantly in the gardens adjoining the ... school in order to recover balls kicked over the walls of the playground' in 1922. For this reason, a wire netting fence was erected. However, when similar wire netting was suggested for the girls' playground, when netball was introduced, the county council turned down the proposal.

Fortunately, in June 1928 Trinity Infants was opened, which relieved a lot of the pressure, and classes were no longer taught in the hall.

The Trinity Schools

The Trinity schools originated in a girls school built in Stallard Street in 1836, next to Trinity Church, which had a capacity of 190. Before 1857 that became a mixed school, and the 150 pupils were taught in two rooms, one above the other. The school was in union with the National Society.

---

2   Each playground apparently also had a tree in the middle, both trees were eventually removed in 1936.

In 1873, Jacob Gayton conveyed a site in Park Street to the vicar and church wardens of Trinity Church and a school was erected for 186 children, boys and infants, called 'Trinity Boys National School'. The total cost of the school was £887, and in 1876 there was still £113:12:8 owing. The vicar and his friends paid most of this, and the parishioners were expected to pay the rest. Cards were prepared for them to pay monthly. The money was gradually obtained and the school on the corner of Park Street started.

By 1877, the number of boys in the school had increased to over 200, the largest number since the school had opened. In 1892, an Infant section was opened on the same site, the boys moving up to the Trinity Boys School at the age of seven, and the girls going to the Girls School in the old Stallard Street building.

However, the opening of the Newtown schools meant, as years went by, that Park Street School was faced by a decline in attendance. The church schools at Park Street and by Trinity Church, however, continued as they were until 1923.

An account of an early school visit undertaken by the boys of Trinity is recorded in the logbook. In October 1919, a party of forty-two boys was taken to Farleigh Castle, following a lesson on the structure of the castle and its history, and the visit was followed by a written composition. A cyclo-styled pamphlet for each boy was prepared, giving an outline of the main features for observation and study. Another visit to the castle in 1923 gave more details of such a visit – the boys had to walk to the castle, and presumably back again!

In 1923, it was decided to amalgamate the church schools at the north and south of the town. Parochial Infants was to stay the same. Boys from the Parochial School were to move to Park Street, and girls from Trinity in Stallard Street were to go to Parochial Girls School. So now all the accommodation at Park Street was for C of E boys, and the Parochial School was just for C of E girls. The infants who had been at Park Street went to the old Trinity Girls building. Because of the proposed amalgamation, Miss Elsie Blanchard, who had been head of the Trinity Girls School since 1915, applied for and was appointed head of Trinity Infants, staying in the same building, of course.

The Parochial and Holy Trinity Schools now came under one united body of managers, under the chairmanship of the Rector of Trowbridge.

The reorganisation of church junior education did not work very well, as the children had to walk further to school. The result was that many children went to Newtown or Adcroft non-conformist schools rather than walk long distances across town.

It was decided in 1926 to build a new infants building on adjacent land to the Newtown school, which would provide places for 200 infants in five classrooms. Expenditure of £4,450 was authorised the following year for its construction.

The completion of this new Trinity Infant building meant the infants from Newtown School and from Holy Trinity went to the new school. The old Stallard Street building of Holy Trinity could be closed. It was subsequently used for Sunday schools until 1932, when it was leased to the Ministry of Works for use as a labour exchange. The building is currently used by the Scouts.

The forty-two-year-old Miss Blanchard now moved on to became headmistress of the new, combined Trinity Infant School.

When Miss Blanchard had become head of Holy Trinity, it had been commented that, 'The present Head Mistress, who had no previous experience of Infant teaching when she took charge in January 1923 [of Holy Trinity], has taken great pains to fit herself for her new task and has made a most promising start. She teaches the first class with success, keeps herself in close touch with work throughout the school.' In later life, Miss Blanchard was described as being around 5'6" tall, slim, grey haired with rather a dark complexion.

The *Wiltshire Times* of 9 June 1928 wrote: 'the infants will be accommodated in an airy, well-lighted school under much better conditions than formerly'. The classrooms opened onto an open verandah. This later provision proved a problem on occasion. In July 1932, due to a heavy storm, it was necessary to move from the 'outdoor setting' of the school to the Newtown hall. The draughts coming through the open passageway into the school were such that parents complained that they were responsible for the children's coughs and colds. A year after the school opened, a suitable door to lessen the draughts was proposed. However, the problems still continued. In 1937, the Trowbridge Attendance Committee felt that the unprotected verandahs of the school and the colds that ensued were probably the cause of the low attendance at Trinity School.

The new school was called 'Trowbridge Trinity Infants Council School' (the name Trinity was kept, as the church felt that they were losing their infant school to Newtown), and had accommodation for 200 children. The school had been built by Mssrs Holdoway of Westbury. Miss Hartley, former head of Newtown Infants, joined the staff, but eventually retired at the age of sixty in 1931. A very interesting insight into the infant education which had previously taken place is revealed with the instruction to the new school that 'children under the age of four were no longer to be admitted'.

The playing area was not all it might have been. The unasphalted portion of the playground was eventually let as an allotment because the ground was so rough, and shrubs, etc. would have been too expensive. However, an edging a yard wide was kept as a flower border. Eventually part of the 'allotment' was used by the Newtown Senior School for 'instruction in Gardening' from September 1932.

Meanwhile, at the Newtown School the 20th century was arriving. The headmaster asked permission to erect a wireless set in the school in July 1924. However, complaints about inadequate lighting in the hall just led to the installation of new gas burners in 1925. Interestingly, the Newtown Infant classrooms did not have gas burners until some years after.

A fascinating insight into one staff issue of the day appeared in the managers' minutes of 1923. In the interests of having a balance of male and female teachers, a female teacher judged to be the least efficient was given notice in order to make way for a male teacher. However, the male replacement was to resign the following year.

If a female teacher married, then the managers had to decide whether to continue to employ her. Following one such case the managers raised no objection to the teacher retaining her post for a time, 'provided the efficiency of her work is not interfered with as a result of domestic affairs'. Subsequent changes in county council policy meant that such discretion was removed from the managers, and until the Second World War, under the terms of their appointment, marriage for women teachers invariably meant their enforced resignation.

The reasoning behind this seemed to be that since there would be considerable unemployment amongst young male teachers who were about to complete their training, it was not right to employ married women teachers who were not dependent upon their earnings as teachers.

Being a woman teacher did have some advantages, however. In May 1937, it was recommended that a disused cloakroom in Newtown be converted into an indoor lavatory for the 'women members of staff'.

From the Newtown logbook there is also an account of a rare educational visit from this period. On 29 June 1929, seventy-one scholars from Newtown left Trowbridge station at 8:45 on the GWR train for Bristol, arriving at 9:30. They first went to the art gallery and the museum in the morning, and then in the afternoon were taken to the Clifton Gorge and the Zoological Gardens. They caught the 6:15 train from Bristol and arrived at Trowbridge after a very long day at 7:15 p.m.

The end of an era came on 31 July 1929. William Hodgson, who had been the head of Newtown since the inauguration of the school in 1898, retired. His last comment in the school logbook was: 'Here endeth the Hodgesonian Dynasty'. He had been head for thirty-one years. He had been a strong character with a great love of music.

Ernest Hughes from Westbury was appointed to succeed him. He was soon faced with a major crisis. In early December that year, a pupil died of diphtheria. Diphtheria in those days was one of the most common fatal childhood diseases. The school was closed for three days to be disinfected. All the classrooms, corridors, cloakrooms, the hall and offices were treated. The school remained closed until 7 January. After briefly reopening, the school was again closed. The exercise books and needlework of those children who had been infected with the disease were burnt in the school furnace. It was not until 29 April that the school finally reassembled. However, the threat of the disease was to linger for years over the school, and was a constant source of worry.

Another New School in the Newtown Area

In 1927, the Sisters of St John of God opened a small school of just eleven pupils – four Catholics and seven non-Catholics – in an old tin hut that had been erected next to the church in Wingfield Road. Eventually this hut was dismantled, and a new private school was opened on the site in January 1936.

St John's, at this point, was an all-age school. With the 1944 Education Act, the school became a junior school, and in 1950 the school was granted aided status, and became a state school. The influx of Polish children with the closing of the Polish school at Steeple Ashton meant a large increase in numbers. Shortage of space in the St John's building in the 1960s meant that for several years classes from St John's shared the Park Street building with those from Newtown.

Reorganisation

To return to the Newtown/Trinity story. As a result of the Hadow Report in 1931, Wiltshire reorganised its schools into primary and senior schools. At the age of eleven, children went to senior school. Newtown was designated as the senior school for that end of the town, and became a Senior Mixed School.

The village schools, which had previously been all-age schools, now lost all their children over the age of eleven, who either went to the nearest senior school or to a grammar school following an exam at eleven. Nearby village schools sent their senior children to Newtown if they were in that area. Children came to the school on buses, whose journeys were sometimes disrupted by adverse weather conditions. However, there were doubts expressed as to the suitability of the Newtown building for senior education. An HM Inspectors report of 1933 commented: 'The accommodation is taxed beyond its capacity for Senior School purposes.'

At Park Street there were changes as well. In September 1931, the school was transferred to the LEA, the Holy Trinity managers decided to lease the premises for twenty-one years to the Education Committee. The school was opened as Trinity Junior Council School for boys and girls. Conditions in the school were crowded; by 1937, two of the six classes were taught in the same room. The head was Mr William Dyke-Meek, who had been head of the Park Street School since 1926. He was a very academic man with very high standards. Mr Dyke-Meek had rather an unbending manner. He had grey frizzy hair. He had a very straight ram-rod back, and stood around 5'8" tall. He would cycle to school daily from his house on Trowbridge Road, Bradford on a very upright bicycle.

In April 1934, William J. Mann, who had presided over the opening ceremony of Newtown School in 1901, and had been chairman of the managers of all the council schools in Trowbridge since 1904, finally retired. He died in the winter of 1936/37.

Changes too were happening at Trinity Infants. In April 1934, a photograph of the children making a new pond appeared in 'The schools at work', a National Union of Teachers publication. The following year, two large additional classrooms were built on either end of the school, to increase the number of classes to seven. The classroom next to the hall was one of these. It was intended as a 'babies' room and had shelving for them to sleep on. The current step in the corridor leading to the Trinity Hall marks the original end of the Trinity building.

Christmas was always greeted with great delight at the school, particularly by the head, Miss Blanchard, who had a great fondness for the festival.

In 1937, there was another interesting proposal. Miss Blanchard suggested that a woman adult patrol be used to safeguard the children crossing the Newtown Road.

Back at Newtown, part of Trinity Infants grounds, which had been used as an allotment, was put to use 'for the instruction of Gardening' from September 1932, and in January 1935, a Mr Cox gave the school a garden at the bottom of the boys' and girls' playgrounds, for the children to use for gardening. Then, in April 1938, the side garden was obtained. In October that year, flowering bushes and trees were planted in this side garden. When cultivating this side garden, a spring was discovered that had to be piped away.

The 20th century finally caught up with the school, when the children returned on 5 September 1938 to discover electric light had been installed in the hall and cloakrooms during the holidays.

The Second World War

1939 saw the start of the Second World War. At the infant and junior schools, the children came to the school premises to be fitted with gas masks. When forty children were evacuated to the junior school, all the teachers volunteered their services as billeting officers. Trinity Infants sent stock to Bethesda Sunday School, which was being used as an infant school for evacuees.

The infant school itself was prepared for the expected air raids. The school was sandbagged soon after the start of the war, and in July 1940 two shelters were erected, each to hold fifty children. Air raid practices were held regularly. By October that year, the children of Newtown Senior School and Trinity Infants could be under cover in their appointed places in two minutes in an air raid drill.

One benefit came from these preparations. In April 1940, the Trinity verandah was enclosed. This was viewed as a 'great improvement' which added 'considerably to the comfort of the school'.

Changes of another sort came to the senior school on a minor level. On 21 May 1940, the girls went for swimming instruction for the first time at the town swimming pool.

On a more significant level, the evacuation of children from London was to mean major reorganisation in the senior school. On 31 May, Newtown became Newtown Senior Boys Council School. The girls went off to be taught in Trinity Church Hall and Bethesda Sunday School. Three weeks later, the Hammersmith School of Building began a move to Trowbridge, and by the end of June there were 243 local boys and 66 evacuees in the school.

Further Reorganisation

However, this was just the start of a much more major change. In 1940, Newtown was to become a Junior Mixed School, and new secondary schools for 400 boys and 400 girls were built on the Galley Farm site on Frome Road, the Nelson Haden Schools (Boys and Girls). These schools were to take children over the age of eleven from the whole of Trowbridge. Ernest Hughes, head of Newtown Senior School, became the new head of Nelson Haden Boys School. Miss V. Ruth Pickett, the head of Adcroft Senior Girls School, was appointed the head of the Nelson Haden Girls School. Until June 1933, Miss Pickett had been a member of staff at Newtown. (Ernest Hughes subsequently became Chairman of Trowbridge Urban District Council 1949–51.)

Books, stationery, smaller items of furniture and school equipment were conveyed to the new schools from the former Newtown Senior School by older children on 11, 12 and 13 September, whilst a van took the bigger furniture on the 13th. Unfortunately, the work of transferring all this was hampered by rain, the muddy state of the approaches to the schools and by air raid alarms.

As most of the rooms to be occupied were not completed by this date, most of the furniture and stock had to be left outside the building or where floor space was available in the various places inside.

The children, books and equipment from Trinity Junior School at Park Street were to come down to the Newtown building under their head, Mr Dyke-Meek, leaving the Park Street building empty. Throughout much of the Second World War it was to be used as an army barracks, particularly by American troops

This move had been planned for some time. For example, Mr Dyke-Meek had been responsible for planning the layout of the trees and bushes along the frontage of the Newtown building in February 1939, over eighteen months before Trinity Juniors actually moved down to Newtown.

Mr Meek commented in the school logbook on 18 September in the Newtown building, 'The first day at Newtown School. It will take a few days to get straight as so much superfluous furniture was left behind.'

In wartime new furniture was at a premium, and throughout the war at least some of the original desks from when the school opened were still in use, and some were still in use in the hall in 1947. As well as these iron-framed desks, there were also more modern wooden double desks with a space underneath into which books, etc. could be slid.

Diphtheria, which had been a constant threat earlier in the century, was finally conquered by inoculation. Two hundred and ten children in Newtown Junior School received their final injection against diphtheria in 1941.

However, there were other threats. Mr Meek wrote in the logbook in April of that year: 'Owing to the Air Raids on Bath, and dropping bombs in this vicinity, sleep of the children much affected, and the reaction to school work was slowed down.'

That was not the only disruption that the education of children at Newtown suffered. In September 1942, presumably as part of the 'Dig for Victory' campaign, the school was closed officially for potato picking. Less pleasant was the ban on central heating to conserve fuel, which resulted in cold classrooms and discomfort for the children in the autumn and winter of that year.

An interesting reflection on the times is shown by the fact that one of the major war efforts by the children was for the Overseas Tobacco League. During the war, £220 was raised by the school to supply servicemen with cigarettes.

A major change in school life that was to outlive the war began in November 1942. Hot dinners were supplied for the first time from a centre in Holt, so that mothers on war work would be able to feel that their children were receiving some warm food. Fifty-six meals were provided, eighteen of these for infants from Trinity.

Life had its light relief, however. As part of the Christmas celebrations in the early 1940s, all the Newtown children were taken to the New Kinema in the town to see such films as *Treasure Island, Toytown Parade* and *Gulliver's Travels*.

Also in this period we see a new development in the children's education. In March 1943, a class was taken to McCall's Cloth Factory as part of Geography scheme of work, perhaps the start of learning from first-hand experience.

New Head Teachers

In July 1947, Miss Blanchard retired as head of Trinity Infants, because of 'advanced age of her mother'. She was presented with 'an extremely beautiful silver tea service' amongst other gifts. Miss Edna Hall was appointed to take her place. Miss Blanchard had been head of one or other of the primary-age schools in the immediate Newtown area for thirty-two years.

In 1940, children had stayed on in the Infant School until they were eight. But by 1948, the increasing numbers meant that children had to leave Trinity at the age of seven. For this reason, Park Street was reopened. The old Trinity Junior buildings were hardly ideal. Despite complaints from the head teacher about the lighting many years before, as late as 1954 gas lighting was still in use in the building. The outside toilets were still to be used until it closed finally in 1992 as part of Newtown Junior School.

Mrs Kate Hayward, who was pictured as a teacher with a class of girls in a photograph of Holy Trinity Girls School of 1905 as Miss Kate Watts, was forced to retire through ill health in the summer of 1949, after at least forty-four years' service. She had taught at Trinity and Newtown Juniors, presumably on the closure of the Holy Trinity Girls School. She unfortunately died shortly afterwards.

In 1949, another teacher with long service left the school. Having reached retirement age, Mr Dyke-Meek resigned as head. In November 1949, Mr Ralph Warburton of Rudloe, Box took over as head of Newtown. Mr Warburton was a short, heavily built man with a heavy moustache. He swiftly set about making a number of changes within the school.

Amongst his new ideas was a more formal morning assembly. The children marched into the hall to orchestral music, which included works by Elgar such as the 'Enigma Variations', 'Nimrod' and the 'Dream of Gerontius'.

He also introduced the first school uniform, with maroon blazers for the boys, and maroon knitted cardigans for the girls. Maroon caps with an NJ badge on the front were now also worn by the boys. To complement this, grey ties with maroon diagonal stripes were worn, and the boys wore grey knee-length socks with narrow maroon bands at the top. Up until this time there was apparently no school uniform worn at Newtown.

In January 1950, he called a meeting of parents and the Parent-Teachers association was formed, with the headmaster as chairman. A series of social events followed, as well as information evenings about 11-plus selection and secondary education.

In the summer of that year the first edition of *Newtown Junior Magazine* was produced, which was primarily written by the children, with accounts of trips and interests, but also featured school news as well. This magazine was to continue for at least ten years, until the 1960s.

Mr Warburton was an ex-army officer, and during his time in charge an annual school trip by train to various locations in the summer term became part of school life. A favourite trip of his was to go up to London to see the Royal Tournament, and in 1954, 251 children, parents and teachers went to London for that purpose.

Large groups were also taken to see major educational films. 375 children visited the Regal Cinema to see *Elizabeth is Queen* in 1953, and 425 saw *Everest* in 1954.

It was apparently at this time that the junior school was divided into four house groups for various 'competitive purposes'. The groups were named after four well-known Wiltshire houses – Corsham, Lacock, Longleat and Wraxall.

In an attempt to raise the standard of play and interest in games, the junior school started to run two football teams in 1950. The idea originated with the pupils. The Flower Show Field and Nelson Haden pitches were used for home matches. During that first season the first team made a successful start, beating the only other Trowbridge junior school, Parochial, twice.

What may have been the first Junior Sports Day was also held that year, with most of the girl competitors wearing shorts! A blackboard was used to chalk up the house scores, but a strong crosswind blew this over.

It was also in 1953 that a stage was built at the back of the Newtown hall under the clock, which was used for assemblies and productions. Possibly as a result of this increased interest in productions, the school choir was successful at the Devizes Musical Festival of 1956. The stage was to survive until November 1970, when it was dismantled and removed.

It was also probably during this time that newer double desks, with lift-up lids, were introduced, as the wartime restrictions on furniture were eased. The iron-framed desks were still in use in the mid-1950s in at least one classroom.

In 1953, romance was to blossom at the school. A Miss J.M. Balch and a Mr F.W.P. Stacey came to be interviewed for posts at the school on the same day, where they met for the first time. Both interviewees were appointed. On 28 July 1954, they were married. They were better known latterly as Fred and Mary Stacey.

There was another change of name in the two schools in 1954, when the word 'Council' was replaced with 'County', the junior school becoming the Trowbridge Newtown County Junior School. At that date it had 484 pupils.

A major change at this time was the appointment of deputy heads to the two schools, following the Burnham Salary Award. At Newtown Senior School, Miss E.M. Cox had been acting head way back in 1934, and Miss M.B. Thomas had been senior mistress in 1946. The latter had been succeeded by Mrs Bessie Rodway in 1952. At Trinity, Miss S.E.M. Cook had been senior mistress in the 1940s, followed by Miss D.M. Howard until 1952, when Mrs Winifred Sleightholme took over the role. In the mid-1950s the role of deputy head was introduced in primary schools. In 1955, Mr J.R. Napthene had been deputy head, but this seems to have been an internal appointment, for with the coming of Burnham national pay and conditions, Mrs Rodway was appointed deputy head. At Trinity, Mrs Sleightholme became the first deputy head.

Another significant change was when Newtown's first clerical assistant was appointed in May 1956, a Mrs R.E. Matthews.

Epidemics, which had been a serious threat to the Newtown School earlier in the century, were still a concern. In 1952, a member of staff was excluded when his daughter contracted polio. Asian flu caused many staff absences in September and October 1957. Polio continued to be a threat until widespread inoculations; 241 children at Newtown were given polio injections in June 1961.

New Schools Open

The building of the Studley Green Estate in the late 1940s and early 1950s caused major problems, as the Newtown School grew and grew in size. There were nearly 200 children at Park Street, one class once totalling fifty-two. In 1955, a new class was added at the Bethesda schoolroom as the number on roll rose to 501. In September 1957, the number peaked at 509 on roll. A similar situation had developed at Trinity, of course, and the Wesley Road schoolroom was put in to use once more in the summer term of 1956. In April 1960, Studley Green School was opened and 130 children transferred to the new school.

Perhaps it was the drop in expected numbers that enabled the creation of a staffroom at Newtown for the first time. The small classroom No. 2, which had originally been designed for an infant class, now became the first staffroom in 1959.

In May 1964, Mr Warburton resigned, having reached retirement age. In January 1965, a new head, Mr John Hicks, from Torrington, Devon was appointed. Mr Hicks was a large, burly and mercurial individual who always put the children first. During the war he had served in the air force. At his interview he had been asked what changes he would make to the school, to which he had replied that he would build a swimming pool.

Among the changes he introduced was that the major trips were no longer whole school outings, but were limited to just one year at a time, the second-year classes going to Beaulieu for example.

In March 1965, Mrs Sleightholme, the head of Trinity, reported to the managers that there was a possibility of employing 'auxiliary non-teaching helpers' in some larger infant schools. In view of the rapidly increasing number in Trinity, permission to appoint such a helper was sought.

This permission was granted, and Beryl Haydock was recruited for the post, apparently the first such to be employed in Wiltshire. She was to stay at Trinity for some twenty-six years, finally retiring in September 1991 with the title of senior care assistant.

John Hicks followed through with his commitment made at his interview. An annual school swimming sports day at the Town Pool was introduced for the juniors, and in the 1967 Easter holidays a school pool was erected by Mssrs Dando and Dack of Midsomer Norton, in what had been the gardening area at the bottom of the playground.

Other changes began to appear. In July 1968, two mobiles were brought in sections to the playground abutting the allotments at the side of the school and taken into use. The allotments themselves were eventually purchased, cleared and made into a playing field in February of the following year, and in August work commenced on extensions to the boys' and girls' cloakrooms, including lavatories in the main school building. However, it was not until April that these were to be taken into use.

It was at this time that new staff toilets were built, taking up part of the large classroom on the left-hand side at the back of the school, next to the head's office. The former cloakroom and lavatory, on the other side of that central block, were converted into a kitchen and a small storeroom.

From 1962, the spare rooms at Park Street were used by classes from the Trowbridge College of Further Education and a class from St John's Catholic School, the latter in the classroom next to the lane. This continued until increasing numbers made it necessary for the classroom to be used by Newtown School itself. The last St John's School class left in July 1967.

By now, Newtown needed the extra classroom themselves. Numbers had begun to build up again and by September 1969 there were 429 on roll. It was then that the Grove School opened, and thirty children transferred to the new school.

These fluctuations in numbers also affected Trinity, and the new head who arrived in 1968, Mrs E. Joan Doel, had to cope with the changing requirements in staffing levels.

In late 1969, there was a major national dispute involving teachers all over the country. The full-time members of staff of Newtown County Junior came out on strike for a fortnight in December that year.

In 1970, Dorothy Amor was appointed as the first Welfare Assistant at Newtown Junior School. Hers was apparently the first such post in Wiltshire. She was to remain as Welfare Assistant for some fourteen years, retiring in November 1984.

The 1970s also saw Trinity Infants grow in size and eventually there were twelve classes, two of them in the Trinity Hall. If a hall was needed, the big end classroom, which was later to be demolished because of subsidence, was used as a hall. For special events like a nativity play, children had to be taken to the Boys Scout Hut along the back lane behind the houses on the eastern side of Newtown. The opening of the Grove School with its drop in numbers eventually meant that the hall was once more available for its original use.

Residential Visits

On 3 May 1971, a major innovation was introduced that was to have a big impact on the junior school, particularly its oldest pupils. Forty-eight children from the fourth year were taken on a five-day residential visit to London, accompanied by Mrs Penny, Miss Smith, the deputy head, Mr Bush and Mr R.P. Stacey. At the same time, Mr Hicks took ten boys for a five-day visit to the Wye Valley.

In 1973, the first residential visit to Swanage took place, and then in 1976 this was extended to include children from the third year, who were taken to St Briavels in Wales. This obviously involved heavy commitment by the staff, some of whom were going to both Swanage and St Briavels during this period.

In 1974, there was a major change in the transfer procedures to the secondary schools, with the end of the 11-plus exams. The Nelson Haden Schools became the Clarendon School, and the High School became John of Gaunt School. Both were comprehensive schools.

By September 1976, the numbers at Newtown were 355 on roll in the eleven junior classes, when 28 transferred to the new Holbrook School when it opened.

In 1977, parties to celebrate the Queen's Silver Jubilee were held in the playground at Park Street and Newtown, and celebration mugs were given to the children.

In April 1982, John Hicks retired as headmaster of Newtown Junior, and Mr Tim Hill, formerly head of Horningsham School, on the Longleat estate, was appointed head. Tim Hill had family connections with Trowbridge, his grandfather used to run a tailor's shop in Roundstone Street.

During his time as head, Tim Hill disposed of the wooden double desks with lift-up lids, and wooden chairs and cupboards which had been in use since at least the 1960s, and replaced them with more modern grey or mushroom-coloured tables with chipboard tops covered in plastic and metal legs, plastic chairs with metal legs, and plastic-covered units.

The 1980s also saw a new head teacher at Trinity, when Mrs Veronica Parker arrived in 1984. She was to make a big impact on the school, seeking to upgrade the furnishings and equipment.

In December 1984, Tim Hill resigned as head of Newtown to become a lecturer in Education at Bristol University School of Education. One of his last acts as head was to restore the bell high in the roof of the Park Street Annex. He and caretaker Bryan Amer climbed up to the small belfry, oiled the bell and attached a rope. The bell had not been rung for over half a century.

Myra Green, formerly Smith, became acting head until April of the following year, when Richard Craft, formerly a deputy head at the John Bull Primary School in Blackheath in London, took over as headmaster. The initially bearded Richard Craft was keen on physical fitness, having previously run a marathon.

Increasing Co-operation Between Trinity and Newtown

The following year saw a marked increase in the interaction between Newtown and Trinity Infants. In May there was a concert at the Civic Hall in which Trinity and Newtown took part, along with Parochial and Margaret Stancomb.

Soon after, Mrs Senior of Trinity and Mrs Harris from Newtown swapped classes for a time.

In 1986, fifty years after Trinity, the juniors finally dug their own pond in the former garden, close to the swimming pool.

In 1989, the partnership process between the two schools moved along still further with another joint concert, and also a joint staff meeting of the two schools.

February 1990 saw a disaster for the Infants School. One of the pratten huts was destroyed by a fire which did £50,000-worth of damage. Six fire crews from Trowbridge, Bradford on Avon, Melksham, Westbury and Warminster were called to tackle the blaze, which started in a store shed and spread to the nearby classroom. Thirty-five firemen were involved in fighting the fire. Flames were apparently leaping into the sky when the firemen arrived, but the fire was under control within twenty minutes. At the height of the blaze roads in Newtown were closed off for more than two hours.

Computers, books and furniture were destroyed in the fire and by smoke and water damage. The school had been on half-term holiday, and when the children returned, two classes had to be taught in the Trinity Hall, and a third was based in the Newtown Junior building.

Twenty-three years after the junior school pool was built, in March 1990, a trench was dug for a gas pipe to the pool area for a boiler to heat the water, and by 30 April the new heated pool was in use. Swimming in water temperatures of 60° F was a thing of the past!

Soon after, Newtown was to lose one of its mobile classrooms. This reduction in the number of teaching spaces could be accommodated because in September the number on roll dropped from 290 to 230, when Walwayne Court School opened on Broadmead. With the fall in numbers in both schools, and the resignation of Mrs Veronica Parker as head of Trinity, the possibility of an amalgamation between Newtown and Trinity became a reality. With the opening of Walwayne Court, the numbers on roll in the two schools were apparently 229 at Newtown and 124 at Trinity. (This compared with a capacity of 335 and 232.)

In June 1991, former Newtown head John Hicks died of a heart attack whilst swimming in Bradford swimming pool. Swimming had always been important to him, and many children had learned to swim at Newtown because of his brainchild, the school pool.

In November of that year, the Trinity governing body made it clear that unless there was a physical link between the two schools, they would be unwilling to support the amalgamation. They felt that without such a link, Trinity would become a mere annex.

In the meantime, Richard Craft was seconded to be head of Holbrook Primary School in 1992. At this time there was also a major change in the way schools were funded, with the introduction of much greater delegation through the Local Management of Schools (LMS).

In July 1992, the Park Street annex finally closed as a part of Newtown School as a result of the continued fall in numbers. However, it was soon to come into use again, this time as Trinity Education Centre, 120 years after it had first opened as Trinity Boys National School.

During the summer holidays of 1992, there were major building works at the back of the Newtown building. The old kitchen and storeroom were replaced with a cooking/teaching area, and the rest of the central block became new staff toilets and a caretakers' room. The classrooms at the back of the building were enlarged. The two small classrooms, formerly the infant classrooms built in 1905, on the right-hand side of the school, were knocked into one large classroom, and the staff toilets were removed from the large classroom on the other side of the school, returning it to its original size.

A new administrative milestone was also reached in 1992, when the Local Management of Schools (LMS) became reality at Newtown, and a cheque for £20,700 was paid into the newly opened Portman account.

In 1992, it was decided to amalgamate Newtown Junior and Trinity Infant Schools. The post of head was advertised, and after stringent interviews, Richard Craft was appointed as head of the new amalgamated primary school. Anne Carter, the deputy of Trinity Infants, and the current acting head of that school, was appointed deputy head.

There was a competition to decide the name of the new school, and a vote taken on what the new primary school should be called. The choice had been narrowed down to two, from a total of nineteen which had been suggested.

One was Roger Brown Primary School, the other choice was Newtown Primary School. In February 1993, 492 parents, teachers and pupils voted for the name 'Newtown Primary', and 128 voted for the alternative. Thus the name 'Newtown County Primary School' was chosen.

Early that year, the link building between the two schools was begun, with offices and library being included as a focus partway between the two buildings. A pupil, Natalie Bergnach, won the competition to name the new school, and her prize was to open the new building.

Amalgamation

Amalgamation followed, and the next year was spent developing and consolidating the links between the staffs of the two schools, meshing them into one cohesive unit.

In March 1994, the top year of the new primary school went off on a new residential visit, to Danywenallt in the Brecon National Park in South Wales.

New housing began to be built beyond the Longfield estate and numbers at Newtown began to rise again, until a fifth new primary school was built in 1997, Longmeadow, and once again children from Newtown School, this time just five, went to build the traditions of another school.

That year changes were made to the area at the edge of the field. The wall next to the field was lowered, and then wooden climbing apparatus was constructed in a banked area next to that section of wall in June that year.

In September 1999, the school's name was changed yet again. It became 'Newtown Community Primary School'.

The year 2000 saw Newtown School begin planning for the celebration of its centenary. Since the actual centenary of the laying of the foundation stone came in the holidays, it was decided to celebrate the centenary on 28 June.

A drama day in Victorian costume was held on Friday, 23 June, and the extensive museum of the history of the school which had been created – photographs, maps, plans, notices, adverts, school reports, artefacts, etc. – was opened to former pupils and staff on Monday the 26th.

The 28th saw the re-creation of the procession from the Town Park to the school by pupils, staff and parents in Victorian costume, headed by the Queen's representative in Wiltshire, Sir Maurice Johnston, the Mayor of Trowbridge, Cllr Angela Milroy and Trevor Heeks, the Trowbridge Town Crier, behind a banner designed and created by the children and parents. When the procession reached the school, everyone reassembled in the back playground for a re-enactment of the laying of the foundation stone, with Roger Day, County Drama Consultant, taking the role of Sir Roger Brown. Former pupil, Janet Anderson MP, Minister for Tourism, Films and Broadcasting, also came to be part of the celebrations.

Over the last hundred years or more, the traditions and ethos of many schools have been woven into the strong fabric that is Newtown School, each leaving its own distinctive legacy.

Trinity Girls School came to an end in 1923, Trinity Boys School was adopted by the LEA as Trinity Junior Council School in 1931, for both boys and girls, thus replacing both Trinity schools. This amalgamated school moved down to Newtown in 1940, to become Newtown Junior Mixed Council School.

Holy Trinity Infants had amalgamated with Newtown Infants in 1928, to make Trinity Infants Council School. In 1993, Trinity Infants and Newtown Juniors amalgamated to create Newtown County Primary School.

Over the years children from Newtown have gone to new schools in the town to build the traditions of another school. Staff and pupils and equipment went from Newtown Senior School to begin the Nelson Haden Schools, then came the first of the primaries, Studley Green, to be followed over the years by the Grove, Holbrook, Walwayne Court and finally Longmeadow. There are now ten primary schools in the town, spread like spokes around a wheel. At the hub of that wheel lies the oldest primary school still in its original building, Newtown.

Newtown School has fulfilled the vision of those individuals who generously supported the idea of a new school in Newtown in the late 1890s – 'to play an important part in the teaching of the young of Trowbridge for many generations'. May this role continue well into the new millennium. As some pupils declared on the day Newtown's centenary was celebrated on 28 June 2000, 'I'm coming back for the next one!'

APPENDIX 1:

Head Teachers

The Junior and Senior Schools

Henry (Harry) Moore was appointed head of Trinity Boys National School when it opened in 1873 in the Park Street building, and was head for thirty-two years and eleven months, the longest period of service in any of the Trinity and Newtown schools. In April 1906, C.V. Manley from Battersea became head. He was succeeded, somewhat abruptly, by Robert A. Wesley in April 1913. In the autumn of 1926, William Dyke-Meek took over the Trinity Junior School at Park Street

The Trinity Girls School headmistress in 1899 was Sarah J. Banwell, who resigned in 1902 and was succeeded by Kate Alice Wells. She in turn was succeeded by Elsie Blanchard in April 1915.

William Hodgson was appointed to be the head of the Newtown Schools when they were still operating in the Wesley Sunday School hall in 1898. After thirty-one years he retired, and in September 1929 Ernest Hughes took over as head at Newtown, which two years later became a senior school. In September 1940, William Dyke-Meek moved the former Trinity Juniors to the Newtown building when Nelson Haden Schools opened. The school became a Junior Mixed School. Then, in 1949, Ralph Warburton became head. On his retirement in 1965, John Hicks became head. He himself retired in 1982 and was succeeded by Tim Hill. In 1985, Tim Hill became an education lecturer at Bristol University, and Richard Craft was appointed as head.

The Infant Schools

The earliest known head of Holy Trinity Infants was Miss L.H. Gibson, who was head from 1896 to May 1901, when she resigned through ill health. Miss Ellen Holland then took over and was in charge from 1901–02, when she left to get married. She was succeeded by Miss Mary A. Weller, who was head from 1903 until 1922, then Miss Elsie Blanchard took over in early 1923.

Miss Chandler was in charge of the Infants originally when the Newtown School was first formed in the Wesley School rooms in 1898. By 1902, Margaret

Hartley was head of Newtown Infants. When Trinity Infants opened in 1928, Miss Blanchard became head, and Miss Hartley became a member of staff of the new school. In 1947, Miss Blanchard retired and Edna Hall became head. In September 1955, Miss Hall resigned to take up an appointment as lecturer in Divinity at Furzedown Training College, London. In January 1956, Miss Olive Richardson of Soham, Cambridgeshire became head, but resigned less than three years later. In December 1959, the existing deputy head, Mrs Winifred Sleightholme, became head. In 1968, she was succeeded by Mrs E. Joan Doel. Mrs Veronica Parker took over in 1984, before moving on to a school in Bath in 1991. Mrs Anne Carter then became acting head until the amalgamation in 1993, when she became deputy head of the new Newtown Primary School

Newtown in 1900

Newtown School boys 1900

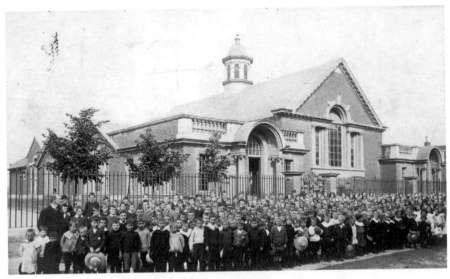

Newtown School the boys 1900

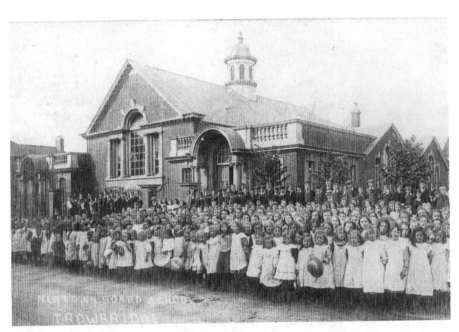

Newtown School the girls 1900

Trinity Boys School circa 1900

Newtown School artist drawing Academy Architecture Magazine 1901

Opening Day - girls

Holy Trinity Girls 1905 Miss Kate Watts later Mrs Hayward on the left

Holy Trinity Girls School

Trinity Boys School 1909

THE 19TH CENTURY

As I have said, the Trinity schools originated in a girls' school built in Stallard Street in 1836, next to Trinity Church. The boys went to Park Street – a school familiar to many children and teachers who attended Newtown.

Memories of Holy Trinity Girls School
By Mary Slade

These reminiscences of Holy Trinity Girls School in the 1870s were written by Bessie Rodway (WSRO -2743/22). The information was given to her by a relative, Mary Slade, who attended the Holy Trinity Girls school during those years. Bessie Rodway was given the information when she started teaching, probably around 1919. Mary Slade took up teaching as a career after leaving Holy Trinity, she became headmistress of a school in Swindon, and received the MBE for her work in the First World War.

At Holy Trinity Girls School, Mary Slade was in a class of 40 children or more. The youngest children or infants were in a gallery in the front of the classroom. Standards 1, 2, 3, and 4 were on the level of the floor. Standards 5, 6, 7 were in the middle of the room.

The staff consisted of one fully trained teacher, one uncertificated teacher and four pupil teachers.

A high standard of education had to be attained in order to get a government grant. Mary Slade said that each teacher had her own method or non-method of teaching. The brighter children often had to teach the slower ones.

The children in third standard learned long division beginning with 13 as the divisor. The work was very thoroughly taught. Each month Miss White, the qualified head teacher, tested each class in arithmetic.

She sat at a table by her desk on the platform. There were four sums on the blackboard of which three were mechanical, and one was a problem. The class stood back to back round the room, slates in arms. As each child finished her work she approached the table on which stood a jar of raspberry drops, a piece of white chalk and a cane. Miss White marked the sums with a capital R if right and a cross if wrong. A sweet was placed on the slate for each correct answer if two, three or four were obtained, but there was no sweet if only one sum was correct and the *cane* if no sums were correct.

A favourite closing hymn was:

The gentle child that tries to please
That hates to quarrel, fret or tease,
That would not say an angry word,
That child is pleasing to the Lord.

Speaking in school to one another was not allowed, caning was the punishment. If a pupil denied speaking and was guilty, she had to face the whole class while they sang:

Ananias was so bold, he a lie to Peter told,
At that moment sad to tell
Dead at Peter's feet he fell –
And his wife who did repeat
Lied like him and crossed his feet

Quick like him struck down in death
Blasted by the Almighty's breath.
Oh! Then as from death you fly
Never dare to tell a lie.
Pray that you in age and youth
May at all times tell the truth.

Mary Slade's mother worked in one of the cloth mills, and had an invalid husband and two children to maintain. She was absolutely determined that her two children should be educated.

When the monthly arithmetic test took place Mary was not allowed to eat her raspberry drops but had to take them home to show her mother as proof of how many sums she had right. On one occasion she was only able to take home three raspberry drops instead of the usual four. She was very frightened to face her mother's displeasure.

Memories of Trinity Boys National School
By Albert Keates

To judge from the names mentioned, the events took place around 1889. The text also gives previously unknown information about an earlier Trinity Girls head teacher, Miss Hill. The logbooks for the school only go back to 1899.

This piece is taken from a longer description of Bradford Road in the early 1880s, written in 1958. The two Trinity schools, for boys and girls, were both Church of England, and all the pupils and staff would attend Trinity Church to celebrate such occasions as Ascension Day, etc. It was transcribed by Albert Keates' daughter, Elsie, who was a pupil at Newtown School in the 1920s.

… at the Trinity Girls' School … all the girls began and finished their education. The boys also received their education here from about four or five years of age until they were six or seven years' old when they were transferred to the Trinity Boys' School in Frome Road (Park Street corner) where they came under the care of Mr Harry Moore and his splendid team of assistants, the chief of whom was Mr John Gardiner. Others were Mr Harry Gerrish, Mr Harry Green, Mr Bert Green and Mr Charlie Green. [Ed. – Harry and Herbert Green were pupil teachers].

The Greens were brothers and their parents were mine host and hostess of the Bell Inn in Newtown. There was one other assistant teacher a Mr.Stokes who lived with his parents and one other brother, Ralph, in the last house of Pilewell Terrace, Newtown – the one nearest to Frome Road.

Mr Moore was also at that time the organist at Holy Trinity Church, and here is a typical scene on what was perhaps a special day in the life of the Church. I am, as it were, standing by the Bell Inn and on either side of the doorway stand Mr and Mrs Green Senior, both about medium height, of a very fresh colour, and, as were their sons, of a healthy appearance.

The Trinity School procession approaches along Newtown, headed by the Headmaster, Mr Harry Moore and over by the Trinity Church wall, stands the Head Governess Miss Hill, with her assistants and all her scholars. They are all going to a service at Trinity Church but the boys from Frome Road enter the church first. The Rev. J.C. Noel, M.A. is the Vicar, the opening hymn being 'Come to the Saviour, make no delay, heed now his blest commands and obey'. The Mr Stokes I have mentioned became the Bandmaster of Frome Town Band in later years.

It was decided in 1926 to construct a new infants' building on adjacent land to the Newtown School, which would provide places for 200 infants in five classrooms.

The completion of this new Trinity Infant building meant the infants from Newtown School and from Holy Trinity went to the new school.

The classrooms opened onto an open verandah. Draughts through the open passageway were such that parents complained that they gave children coughs and colds. In 1937, the Trowbridge Attendance Committee felt that the unprotected verandahs of the school and the colds that ensued were probably the cause of the low attendance at Trinity School.

Memories of Newtown Infants and Mixed Schools
By Elsie Keates

I commenced at Newtown Council School after the Easter holidays in 1917, being then five years of age. The Infants section was in a building at the back of the new school which was opened on the March 1901 to accommodate 400 children. The teachers were Miss Hartley, headmistress, assisted by a Miss Payne, Mrs York – known then as Miss Coles and Miss Phyllis Burnett, who later became Mrs Philip Rose. Miss Burnett took the five-year-olds.

In the Infants and later the desks had iron frames with tip-up wooden seats. The desks were arranged in rows. We did reading and writing and easy sums. I remember drawing a picture of a primrose in chalk and Miss Hartley sending me around the infant classes to show my drawing to the other children.

[At this time Trinity Infants had not been built and the land on which that school would later be built was still allotments.]

I moved into what was known as the 'big' school at the age of seven and the teachers were Miss Giddings, Miss Ethel Cox, Miss Batchelor, Miss Bessie Smith (pupil teacher who later went to college and will be remembered by some as Mrs Bessie Rodway who was their teacher and who died on 30.12.96 at the age of ninety-five), Miss Elsie Holland who took standard 4 – she came from West Ashton on her motorbike – quite a sensation in those days: Miss Ruth Pickett taught standard 5, she was a Girl Guides Captain: Mr Henry Leonard Scott taught standards 6 and 7 in one of the classrooms. There were three classes in the main hall, divided by portable partitions. At the end of each term the classes in the hall moved into the classrooms and vice versa.

In the classrooms the boys would sit on one side and the girls on the other, or sometimes the boys at the front and the girls at the back. Sometimes children were kept back a year to repeat work. By Standard 7 the class was small because many children had left by then. The cane was still in use and used by the teachers on both boys and girls.

Physical Training would consist of stretching one's arms and drill. The classes were mixed for this and it was taken by the class teacher.

Following the calling of the registers all the classes assembled in the main hall where we sang one or more verses of the hymn 'Father, lead me day by day' (during Lent it was 'There is a green hill far away'), followed by the saying of the Lord's Prayer.

The Headmaster was Mr William Hodgson who was very keen on music, and a choir would be entered for the Devizes Music and Drama Festival often winning one of the trophies. Country dancing was also popular and teams would be entered to compete at the festival.

In about 1924 Mr Scott left to become the headmaster at Downton School near Salisbury and he was succeeded by a Mr Fred Foulkes who was not so popular. At some time in the 1920s there was a teacher called Mr Welchman.

At playtimes we would play different games according to the season – conkers, marbles, skipping, jumping over the rope, and hopscotch. We played Stag, where you had to run from one side of the playground to the other. If you were caught you had to touch hands in a line that would gradually spread across the playground.

From the age of eleven to thirteen the girls went on what we used to call our 'Cookery' class each Monday at the Adcroft Girls' School in British Row. It was in fact a full course on domestic science as we learnt not only how to cook, but how to clean a coal burning range including the flues (most of the houses had either a range or gas stove in those days); how to prepare and wash the laundry – by hand, how to clean and polish the silver, etc., etc. How lucky we are today to have so many electric appliances to assist us. Our teacher was a Miss Agnes Eaglesome who lodged at 'Mornington' in Bradford Road and was very well liked.

For the boys it was Gardening at the Palmer Gardens. For an hour or so on one or two afternoons each week the girls did knitting and sewing while the boys went to woodwork classes and I believe these were held at the Adcroft Boys' School in Prospect Place.

I always walked to school from my home in Bradford Road. There was little traffic, only horse and carts.

The only 'outing' I can recollect is a visit one afternoon to the Brickworks which were situated at Upper Studley. I left school at Easter 1926.

I sat the exam for the High School but my mother persuaded me not to stay on to sixteen so I left school at fourteen and spent three months looking for a job. I eventually got one with Wilts United Dairies and stayed there forty-seven years. The firm is now called Unigate, but is still at the same place, opposite what is now the Shires.

Newtown was a happy school with a reputation for good teaching and good behaviour.

Memories from the 1920s and 1930s
By Trevor Bottomley

My first school was Trinity Primary which I attended from age five. At nine we moved to the nearby Newtown Elementary school. Except for the slates and slate pencils which were our only writing materials, and watching the 1927 eclipse through bits of broken smoked glass from the school playground I recall little of significance about my primary schooling.

But I remember Newtown school with affection. It was a modern, rather grand, building in Edwardian style, for both sexes, though boys and girls sat in their own groups in class and each had their own playgrounds. We began each day with 'assembly', which in its formality established the strict but tolerant discipline of our school life. At Newtown we used nib pens to write and each desk had its own ink-well which was topped-up each day by an ink-monitor. We also used 'exercise' books, one for each main subject, into which we wrote the blackboard summaries of our lessons and our class 'exercises'. There was no 'homework' but we could take home books from the school library.

The teacher I remember best was a Welshman named Rees. He, as I later realised, had a great love for language and literature which he did his best to transfer to us. He encouraged us to read and to learn and use new words, and would circle in red any he specially approved of in our exercise books. Having found the word 'dexterity' in Stevenson's *Treasure Island* I concentrated hard on working it into my compositions, as our English essays were called. The first time I used it he had me read out the passage to the class and give an explanation as to its meaning. The second time I got a red circle. The third time, when I tried to work it into a poem on 'rain' he said 'A little word like "apt" would be a useful one to learn now, Trevor.' I do not recall him as a strict disciplinarian, though we were never in doubt as to the behaviour expected of us, or of the retribution which might follow any transgression. His classroom was quite steeply stepped so he always had an excellent view of what every member of the class was doing at all times. A cane, used for pointing to the black-board, was always prominently displayed on his desk but I never knew him use it for any other purpose. A friendly clout with your own ruler was the only physical punishment I ever experienced or saw him administer. I can however recall the pain of several visits to the Headmaster's room for 'the cane' when I had fallen foul of the school's rules in some way: though, except for one occasion, I cannot remember in what ways I had been at fault.

The school gardens were on the top of a railway embankment which ran behind the school. One day when we were supposed to be planting potatoes under the supervision of Mr Rees, a classmate we called 'Elmtree' shouted to me, 'Hey, Ginger (my school nickname), chuck us the fork'. Stupidly I did just that and it went into his foot. He was despatched to the clinic and I to the Headmaster for 'two on each hand'.

In retrospect, and from what I hear of contemporary education, it seems to me we followed a quite balanced and progressive curriculum which would have found favour with present-day administrators; though the methods used (effective as they were) would perhaps get less applause.

As well as a thorough grounding in the three 'R's' and other academic subjects there were several other activities. We had two periods of PE each week; although in those days the 'E' simply stood for 'Exercise' and not the grander word 'Education' which is used nowadays. Gardening and games were included in PE, and in the summer we were taught to swim at the local 'baths' – a section of the river upstream of the town where it was not too fouled by the effluent of the factories.

Once a fortnight, in crocodile fashion, we walked halfway across town to the Technical Institute where there were facilities for wood-work for the boys and cooking for the girls. Happily, we were allowed to walk home without supervision which enabled the boys to try their luck in persuading the girls to hand over some of the little cakes they had been making in cookery-class.

As the girls, who had had to take a penny or two to school to pay for the ingredients, were usually under strict instructions from their mothers to take home whatever were the result of these donations we didn't have much luck. Unless, that is, there was some quid pro quo offering in the way of articles made in wood-working class. There was however little scope in that direction as the boys only produced about three articles such as bread boards, letter racks, and egg racks – a year.

The only contemporary disagreement I had with Newtown School was that from my first year I was banished from singing class on the ground that I was tone-deaf, and sent to 'sort out the books' in the library while the others sang. A banishment which, as I liked singing, I always considered very unkind and unreasonable. I could not understand why my rendering of 'Who is Sylvia?' as any less musical than the rest of the class. However, as it meant I became a 'book-monitor' throughout my school career, it helped to develop a love of reading and books. Had I had not been banished I might never have known that the lyric of the song was from a Shakespeare sonnet, or bothered to speculate as to the intriguing answer to the question in the title.

Another teacher I recall with less affection was a Miss Pickett; who later became the Head Teacher of a new secondary school, called Nelson Haden after a local dignitary who had made his fortune installing central heating in Wiltshire's schools. After the war she was the chairman of a county committee for selecting people to be trained as teachers under a post-war emergency training scheme.

In 1946, armed with a recommendation from an RAF education officer (I was by that time a Flight Sergeant, on the point of being discharged from the RAF) I appeared before Miss Pickett's committee as an applicant for training; only to be abruptly, and not too courteously, turned down by my ex-teacher, who clearly thought I was getting a bit above myself. She obviously had far less regard for the education provided by Newtown School than I had.

In my old age I have one severe criticism of Newtown School: we were never taken anywhere! We lived in an area crammed with important historical sites but were never taken to any of them. Bath, with its Roman baths, the beautiful Abbey, and its unparalleled Georgian architecture was ten miles way. We could have walked to the great, medieval, tithe barn at Bradford-on-Avon; and the massive, Norman castle at Farleigh Hungerford. Stonehenge and Avebury were a half-day's journey by bus.

The Kennet and Avon Canal, a defunct relic of the industrial and transport revolution, ran almost past our door. Five miles away, marked by the 'white horse' carved into the chalk of the downs, was the site of one of the most significant battles fought by our own Wessex King, Alfred the Great. We learned about his 'burning of the cakes' but were never taken to the site of his great victory over the Danes at Edington. We were not even taken into the woollen mills where most of us expected to spend our working lives (and most did).

For that matter Trowbridge itself had much in its own history, industry, and architecture of which to be proud; and which could have provided the substance of many an interesting lesson. Not least the precepts, ornately carved in Bath stone, above the facade of the frontal colonnade of the Market Hall: 'A false balance is an abomination to the Lord' and 'Owe no man anything'. Appropriate puritanical reminders to all who passed beneath that to cheat, or seek to deceive, for whatever reason was not the conduct expected in this, primarily God-fearing, non-conformist, radical-liberal community. They well summed up, I suppose, the lessons our teachers in family, school, and chapel sought to impart.

Trowbridge had been the principal centre of the West-of-England woollen industry for over 200 years, and was an important market town with a weekly animal and produce market. It was also the administrative centre of Wiltshire and, apart from County Hall, contained the HQ of many of the county's institutions, including the Wiltshire Yeomanry, a mounted Territorial Regiment. Several gracious, Georgian style, town 'mansions' provided evidence of the wealth derived from the cloth trade; and its Georgian and early Victorian public buildings were appropriate monuments to the civic pride of people who had prospered, a few significantly more than most, in that trade.

At age eleven I took the entrance examination for the local grammar school and, if an interview with the head was anything to go by, passed creditably. However, I was not offered one of the few free places available but my parents were told I would be accepted for three guineas a term. This was almost the equivalent of my father's weekly wage and not therefore practicable. My mother was very unhappy at this outcome but, except that he suspected some discrimination had been exercised, my father wasn't much concerned as he hoped and intended that I would be apprenticed in his trade.

In any event, my contribution to the brief family conference on the matter was to forcibly reject the idea of staying at school until age sixteen. To this day I can only admire my childish perspicacity. Had I gone to the grammar school I might well have become (perish the thought) a local government officer, or even a teacher! And these memoirs would have told a far different story.

[Ed. - Instead Trevor became a Co-operative development expert, visiting more than fifty countries and working at one point for the Ministry of Overseas Development. He wrote a book *Happy Highways*, his autobiography (ISBN 1 903341 54 X).]

THE 1930s

As a result of the Hadow Report in 1931, Wiltshire reorganised its schools into primary and senior schools. At the age of eleven, children went to senior school. Newtown was designated as the senior school for that end of the town, and became a Senior Mixed School.

At Park Street there were changes as well. In September 1931, the school was opened as Trinity Junior Council School for boys and girls. Conditions in the school were crowded; by 1937, two of the six classes were taught in the same room.

Trinity Infants and Trinity Junior in the 1930s
By James Carter

I started school at Trinity Infants School in 1934 at approximately five years old. I remember little of it, except for one of the teachers was a Mrs York, and my last classroom was a square one, very near the railway lines. Towards the end of my time there a pond was created and it had frog spawn in it and then tadpoles formed, we also had a 'jungle jim' which is now known as a climbing frame – oh! We had fun on that!

I remember in the summer we had small mats, to lay on for a rest period, on the verandah some afternoons.

Alas, bye bye small school, now for the big school Park Street – this was an older school and not so nice, cold at times, with its tall roofs and beams, small playground. Teachers at this time, about 1937 to 1940, were as I remember Miss Joyce (always had her hair in a bun) younger than the other teachers but a firm favourite with most of us!

Mrs Hayward, very strict, I think most of us were a little afraid of her, well I was!

Mrs Beaven – very nice, strict but if you could not understand something and found it hard to do she would stand by your desk and help you along, and usually it all worked out!

Mrs White took the top class, I think children today would call her super.

Sometimes during the war, if we were at play, we would see a convoy of tanks or army lorries going along Frome Road, causing great excitement.

Playtime in the morning we had a third of a pint of fresh milk in a small milk bottle and a straw to drink through – free as far as I can remember.

If we had any pocket money left we could also buy two small ginger biscuits for a penny or one Polo biscuit for a penny, it was a wheat biscuit with chocolate on one side, this was a real treat!

Mrs White's classroom had a glass-wooden partition down one side, which would slide back to make a larger room for morning prayers and assembly, hymns were usually 'Jerusalem' or 'He who would valiant be'. Pupils always faced the blackboard in rows, sat at our desks and we never moved around.

First lesson was always 'Scripture' training a psalm, or a verse, or a story from the Bible.

After Park Street it was off to Newtown Senior School for a while, then off to a lovely new school, Nelson Haden School [Clarendon] but that's another story.

The Recollections of Norman and Kenneth Rogers (Trinity Infants School 1935–38 and Park Street/Newtown Junior School 1938–41)
By Norman Rogers

I was born on 14 September 1930 in Dursley Road, one of twin brothers. My twin brother and I joined Trinity Infants School in April 1935 when we were just over four and a half. The building consisted of two wings at right angles; the one parallel with Newtown had two classrooms, the other three. The wings enclosed a playground and on the playground side was a verandah. At the angle were the cloakrooms (i.e. where we hung our coats) and the washbasins. On the first floor was the staff accommodation. The only time I went upstairs was when we went for our preliminary interview. The entrance was across a narrow playground. To the right as you crossed the playground were the outdoor toilets, boys' and girls'.

When I first joined the school, two extra classrooms were being built, a new 'babies class' to the left of the main playground as you face away from Newtown, and a room joined on to the end of the other wing. I seem to remember a steam excavator and the workmen laid a narrow-gauge rail track from the entrance to the new building on the left with a little turntable at the corner and used to push their material in tiny side-tipping trucks. I think that, at this time too, they laid out the senior playground.

TEACHERS: The staff was entirely female. The Head was known as the 'Governess'.

The 'Governess' (Head) was Miss Blanchard. She lived in Newtown, a few doors from the school. She had a room at the top of the stairs at the right of the entrance. I remember going up to see her with my mother and my brother, possibly when we went to see about joining the school.

Other teachers included: Miss Paul, who took the 'babies class' (not yet dignified by the name of 'reception') when I first joined the school, Miss Say, an elderly lady with iron-grey hair and a bun who took the next class up, Miss Usher, Miss Cook, sister of the famous scientist, Sir William Cook; she lived with her father in Drynham, Mrs York, who took the senior class and who lived in Bradford Road.

All lived locally, within walking distance. I was taught by all those I have named. As I spent three years and one term in the school, I must have spent less than a year with some, although I was in Mrs York's class (the top class) for a whole year. In September 1935, the 'babies' class was transferred to the new detached classroom, with Miss Howard in charge. In the last year, the year group was split into two streams, Mrs York taking the top stream in the other new classroom. This was called Standard One.

I began in the 'babies' class in room 4 on the plan with Miss Paul. Later we transferred to room 1 with another teacher whose name I cannot remember. This was the only room without rows of desks. There were toys and objects hanging around the walls with name cards. Next, I spent some time with Miss Say in room 2. On the wall of Miss Say's class was a poster saying 'Tea and coffee go away/Milk and cocoa come to stay' with pictures of a teapot and a coffee pot with arms and legs running away and a similar milk bottle and cup of cocoa running towards you.

After that we were in room 3 with Miss Usher and I remember while standing in a group reading aloud, suddenly realising that s-a-i-d formed the word 'said'. We had a period of rest in the afternoon, lying on coconut mats and pretending to be asleep. Then, as in most of my adult life, I found it entirely impossible to sleep in the day. One of the teachers got married, possibly Miss Usher, and was presented with a green bedspread as a wedding present. I remember it being shown to the assembled school.

Next, I was in Miss Cook's class. she had a reputation for being strict. In this class, I remember, certain children were dosed with cod-liver oil. They each had to bring a spoon to school. I was very glad not to be one of them. (One girl died of TB during our time there). We paid 2d a week for milk and drank ⅓ pint a day from tiny bottles with cardboard tops. In Miss Cook's class we used the tops to decorate the cover of a little writing book we made and in which we wrote word lists (spellings). I still have it.

I remember writing with chalk on slates – all our writing was 'script', i.e. not joined up.

We were also able to contribute to National Savings, our payments being entered on a card and eventually we received a certificate.

We did various forms of painting. Sometimes we painted figures or objects which were pasted on a long strip of sugar paper and pinned up round the classroom as a frieze – one was devoted to autumn with a bonfire and brown leaves.

Another thing we did was to draw a hedgerow with trees in the foreground on a piece of paper, then a row of hills, the rest of the page being the sky. Then a colour was chosen, say pink. The foreground (the hedge and trees) was painted three times, the hills twice and the sky once so that there were three depths of colour – very simple but effective. We also had 'drill' in the playground. How long I spent in these classes I do not know, but it must have been less than a year in some. Most children were respectably dressed, but a few came in little more than rags and not particularly clean ones either

My last year was in Mrs York's class in room 7. This was a large room with a terrace overlooking the garden of Newtown Senior Elementary School or Newtown British as it was often known. In the winter we were encouraged to grow hyacinths, the best to get a prize, but the plan misfired as I think that the school was closed as a result of an epidemic of some childish illness and by the time we resumed school the flowers were over. I think we all had a small Easter egg as a consolation prize. We also had some kind of a test, possibly an intelligence test, in which I came 20th in a class of about fifty children. We were stood in a line around the room in order of achievement. We learnt about sugar cane and sugar production and Mrs York asking whether we believed that you found a little bag of sugar at the top of the cane.

We did 'drill' in the new playground next to the railway and there was a climbing frame called 'Jungle Jim'.

We went to school unaccompanied from an early age, because there was little in the way of traffic and a lot of it slow horses and carts. At lunchtime and at the end of the day we were marched in a column up to the main road and the teacher saw those who lived on the opposite side across the road.

Classes were large (when I revisited the school a few years ago, an old register was on display for my class and there were forty-three boys and girls). From Miss Say's class onward, we sat in rows of double desks with a tippable seat joined to the heavy iron framework. These were standard throughout the two schools except in Mrs York's class which was in a more modern room, so we had double desks like little tables, with a space for books underneath and separate chairs. Teaching was formal and discipline was enforced. Miss Say and Miss Cook certainly brooked no nonsense.

In September 1938 we moved to Trinity Junior School in Park Street. This was also an L-shaped building. In the wing parallel to Park Street there were two rooms separated by a retractable wooden and glass screen. The wing parallel to Frome Road also had two rooms separated by a similar screen. One end of this room was large and so was divided again by movable canvas screens about five foot high. Between this wing and Frome Road were the boys' entrance and cloakroom and an extra classroom. At the angle of the L was the staff room and the girls' cloakroom was at the far end of the Park Street wing. The boys' playground was adjacent to Frome Road and the girls' in the angle of the L.

There were three year groups each divided into A and B streams. Miss Rogers (no relation) taught standard 2A on one side of the canvas screen; Mrs Beaven taught 2B in the extra classroom; Miss Thomas taught 3A in the middle classroom of the other wing; Mrs Hayward taught 3B on the other side of the canvas screen; Mrs Dangerfield taught 4B at the far end of the Park Street wing and Mr Daniel taught 4A at the far end of the Frome Road wing. Classrooms were formally arranged with rows of double desks facing the teacher's desk at the front. Some of the teachers' desks were like the old-fashioned sloping-top school desks, but much higher and with a folding shelf at the side. The chairs were high too, and had a foot rest. In at least some classes, boys sat on one side and girls on the other. Lessons were formal and quiet. We did not play up any teachers, but it was especially important not to get on the wrong side of Mrs Beaven, Mrs Hayward, Mr Daniel and, of course, the Headmaster, W. Dyke-Meek.

No teacher had any compunction about administering a sharp slap and a smack around the ear was not uncommon. You could also be kept in and made to repeat work not properly done. Only Mr Meek used the cane, often in public. I remember one incident in which he wanted to cane a boy and had lost his cane. The unfortunate boy was sent out to Bailey's shop in Dursley Road to buy a cane. On his return, Mr Meek explained that the cane might split in use and that the way to prevent that was to singe the ends; which he proceeded to do with his lighter. Then he caned the boy (probably six). (Mr Meek smoked a pipe and Mr Daniel cigarettes. I cannot remember ever seeing any of the female teachers smoke.)

Trinity being a Church School, religion played a prominent part. We started the day with assembly, in the room parallel to Park Street, with the screen retracted. There was a hymn and prayers. The hymns were all adult hymns and were written in big print on large pieces of cardboard which were placed high on an easel. 'Summer suns are glowing' and 'Let us with a gladsome mind' are two that come to mind. The first lesson of the day was Scripture. We used the Authorised Version of the Bible. I remember copying out 'They that go down to the sea in ships and do business in great waters' ... etc. There were short class prayers at the end of the morning, at the beginning and end of the afternoon.

Various memories of Standard Two with Miss Rogers:

– we had a student teacher and she asked us to bring as many as possible of the squares of tissue paper in which oranges were then wrapped and she hung bundles around the room. Miss Rogers later asked us to bring something (I cannot remember what) and, when the response was nothing like so good, she was very cross she reminded us how different it had been when we brought all those papers that 'stank the place out'.

– towards the end of term we were allowed to bring our own books to school and when we had finished our own, we swopped. I borrowed *The Heroes* by Charles Kingsley which I read avidly. It was my first introduction to Classical Mythology.

– at the end of the day, we had to stand in silence before we were allowed to go. Miss Rogers always said that she wanted to be able to hear a pin drop.

– a conjurer came to the school at Christmas.

– Mrs Beaven took us for handwork. We made paper windmills and a thing that was supposed to make a sharp crack if you brought it down sharply through the air (like lightning produces thunder).

This year always has a special place in my memory as it was the last year of street lamps, lighted shop windows, oranges, bananas and all those things which disappeared with the coming of the Second World War, and many of which I did not see again until I was grown up.

War was declared on 3 September 1939. It was in this month that we moved up into Standard 3A, Miss Thomas's class. The start of the school year was delayed and when, eventually, we returned, we went for only three days a week. I cannot remember how long this arrangement lasted but I think not very long. During this period, and during the major part of the war, Trowbridge had a vast number of air alerts but very few bombs actually fell. At the beginning there were no shelters, so, during this year in Park Street School, if the siren sounded, pupils dispersed to the homes of those living nearby. My brother and I went to a house about halfway along Park Street. Should the parent of the boy who lived there be out, we were instructed to knock at the house next door. This happened once and we were taken in by the very elderly couple who lived next door. We all had gas masks which we took wherever we went, even to school. We had to practise putting them on and wearing them. The main problem was that the eye-piece got steamed up.

Various memories of Standard 3-A:

– we went for nature walks along Silver Street Lane (which then was a country lane with high hedgerows). We picked flowers and fruits and, on our return to school we wrote them up in a nature note book, allotting them to families such as Liliaceae or Amaryllidaceae. Every other page was blank so that we could draw the flowers.

– we had a man supply teacher who read us *The Pied Piper* by Robert Browning. He also taught us the diseases of sheep; I think he confused foot rot with liver fluke. He was, perhaps the son of one of our teachers, Mrs Hayward. Mrs Hayward had been a teacher in this area of Trowbridge for many years. As Miss Kate Watts, she had taught our mother.

– Mrs Dangerfield read us *Treasure Island* by Robert Stevenson. 'It contains a lot of blood and fighting,' she said, 'so I know you'll like it.' Mrs Dangerfield also took us for handwork. I made a castle gate out of stiff paper, complete with portcullis made from matchsticks. I was very pleased with it although Mrs Dangerfield was far from impressed.

– Mr Meek took us for poetry in Mrs Beaven's room. We read 'There are fairies at the bottom of our garden' and one about a toy ship with 'a dolly at the helm'. We copied out the poems in our best handwriting. (We used 'joined up' writing at this stage.) My brother made up a limerick and Mr Meek was so impressed that he made us all produce limericks. Mine was:

> There was a young knight of the Middle Ages
> Who said 'In history, my deeds will go down on pages;
> And people will look
> At their history book
> And say "What a wonderful knight of the Middle Ages".

The teachers addressed us by our Christian names, but Mr Meek used surnames, at least, for boys. He always called my brother, Kenneth Rogers, Harris, because he got him mixed up with Kenneth Harris who was in the same class. Our mother was 'Mrs Harris'.

All this time, I suppose, we were plodding on with our English and

Arithmetic, learning our tables and doing sums and problems, as well as Mental Arithmetic. In this school we were considered old enough to do joined-up writing. We still wrote on slates.

In September 1940 we moved to the top class with Mr Daniel. This was the year of the move to Newtown. Before we moved one incident took place that remains in my memory. In Mr Daniel's classroom was a cabinet of curiosities, including a jar containing a piece of potassium. Mr Daniel took the potassium from the jar and cut it with his penknife to show us how it smoked. Suddenly, it burst into flames and he threw it on the floor. We were sent into the playground (fire drills had not been invented) while the fire was dealt with by the staff. It was quickly put out but left a large burn mark on the floor. When we moved the contents of the cabinet were distributed among the class. I had a piece of Roman tile and my brother a fragment of Samian ware.

The move to Newtown came upon us very suddenly. A new senior elementary school (later known as Secondary Modern Schools) had been finished in Frome Road. At the very beginning it was known as 'Galley Farm School', later Nelson Haden and now Clarendon. At this time, just after the evacuation from Dunkirk, the army were desperately short of billets for the troops and had their eyes on any suitable building which they could commandeer. Newtown was considered, by the Education Authority, a better building than Park Street, so we moved out of Park Street and the army moved in and remained there until the end of the war. The boys in the top class had to help. We carried anything that we were capable of along the back lane between the houses in Park Street and those in Newtown leading into Wesley Road and so to our new school. We were, of course, totally unsupervised, but there were very few motor vehicles, petrol being short and strictly rationed and, in any case, we had been going to school on our own for several years. (We were often sent out of school on errands for the teachers.)

Newtown had an assembly hall that Park Street lacked. There were two classrooms on either side of the hall and a further two towards the railway. Mr Daniel's class was in one of the latter. There were two entrances one for boys and the other for girls, and still so marked, I believe, and the appropriate cloakrooms just inside. The lavatories were, of course, separate in the playground. Newtown also had brick-built air-raid shelters. No longer did we disperse to other people's houses to be given cocoa and biscuits. We just sat in the dark, damp shelter, keeping up our spirits by singing or by popping outside if there was a dogfight going on in the sky above us. During that year we spent a good many hours in the shelters.

Newtown also had a garden. Mr Daniel taught the boys gardening. We planted vegetables and learned most of the common tasks. We also maintained the small plots in front of the school. I loved gardening and was most disappointed if we could not go out because of the rain and had to stay in and do garden plans. After the results of the 'scholarship' (later known as the 11-plus) were announced, life in the top class was more relaxed and we would spend whole days working in the garden.

The main event of the year was, of course, the 'Scholarship', the 11-plus exam to select those who would go on to secondary education, i.e. the Trowbridge Boys' and Girls' High Schools. There were two or three papers, a psychological test (shapes to identify, etc.) and English and Arithmetic which may have been taken together in one paper. We sat the papers in the Assembly Hall. There was also an interview conducted by the Headmaster of TBHS, Mr L.G. Smith. The interview was at Newtown School, because of the air-raid alerts; the result was that, the day before I began at the High School, I had to be taken to be shown where it was as I did not know.

Various memories of the year:
– drawing, one afternoon, a picture of Meg Merrilies, following an English lesson in the morning. Meg Merrilies comes in a novel by Scott and a poem by John Keats and it is probably this poem we had read.
– being kept in one lunch time for misspelling 'chief' as 'cheif'. When taken to task, I quoted 'i before e except after c' only to be told 'immediately after'.
– arithmetic (Maths was a secondary school subject) consisted of sums, problems and mental arithmetic. One problem I remember was working out how many tiles would be needed for a bathroom of a certain size. Learning how to reckon in £ s.d. was very important, as were all the Imperial measures of length and weight.
– in English, we learnt how to divide a sentence into subject and predicate.

– one day Mr Daniel asked us to bring some pieces of cloth or flannel. Ken and I remembered and took some flannel and one girl also remembered. He was very cross at the poor response. He had two pieces of ice, one of which he wrapped in flannel and the other was left out in the air. The piece left bare melted first, so we learnt that cloth does not so much keep you warm as insulates you from changes of temperature.

I think we were lucky to go to Newtown School. Academic standards were high, with a very good pass rate for the High Schools. At least twelve boys in our year went and a number of girls, though I am not sure how many. Six went on to University. My parents had no thought of sending us to TBHS, until, one day, Mr Meek came into the room and said, 'Stand up all those who will go to the High Schools if they pass'. My brother and I sat tight. 'Stand up, you two,' said Mr Meek. 'Oh no,' we said, but were brusquely told to do what the Head said. We stood up. That was how it was we went to the High School.

Memories of Trinity Junior School – at Park Street
By Mrs Betty Cox (née Tilling)

I came to Trinity Junior School in 1935 from Trinity Infants School in Newtown. There were forty-six in the class and we sat in double desks with iron frames and bench seats.

The blackboard was on an easel. An ink monitor filled the inkwells which were sunk into the desks. The Holy Trinity Sunday School was also held here, so it was school again on Sunday afternoons.

At first, I was afraid of the playground because there was much shouting and running around. The toilets were outside not much different from the one at home because then many were outside at the bottom of the garden. The boys had a separate playground overlooking Frome Road.

I remember standing at the side railings thinking as I watched the traffic that we were behind bars and not let out. Little did I know that my husband to be was in the nearby playground.

I also remember looking out of the window once when a little biplane went by, and Mr Daniel said 'Stop looking out the window, anyone would think you'd never seen an aeroplane.' Of course, we didn't see many in those days.

The girls wore rather shapeless frocks and flat-bottomed shoes. The hair was mostly parted on the side and tied back with a slide or ribbon. To curl our hair, mothers would wind material around the hair and tie into a knot. Boys would wear rather long shorts and a pullover.

Going to school in the morning, if I had a farthing or a halfpenny, I would call into Roses' shop in Bond Street and buy broken biscuits for lunch time if there was any left by then. We had about an hour for lunch, just time to rush home and have rabbit stew.

One third of a pint of milk in small glass bottles was also given to the pupils.

In my last year Mr Daniel was the teacher. He was short and slim and a Welshman. His discipline was absolute and his temper volatile. He was keen to have us pass the 11-plus and worked us hard. Mr Dyke-Meek, the headmaster, would wander into the classroom and immediately ask questions such as the times table and why is the earth round? He expected prompt answers.

Arithmetic tables were chanted each day and grammar was very important. English, Composition, Language Study, Poetry, Reading, Arithmetic, Geography, History, Art, Nature Study and Needlework or Handwork were all taught. Sewing was for me a disaster, being left handed, smocking was hopeless.

I remember a map of the world on the wall with much coloured pink to show the British Empire. Mugs were given to us in 1937 to commemorate King George VI's Coronation.

Discipline was strict and pupils were sent outside the classroom, hoping the Headmaster was not around.

Our health was monitored by a visit from the school doctor, Dr Jean Murray. A dentist also visited the school and we were dispatched to the local clinic if necessary. The nurse called to check our heads for nits.

Many of us missed a great deal of lessons because of illness. These were the days before immunisation and many of us caught measles, mumps, whooping cough, diphtheria or scarlet fever. If we survived then our immune system was probably very good. I remember one girl died of diabetes. Children who were undernourished were given cod liver oil daily and severely undernourished children were sent to a sanatorium.

The next class to ours was Mrs Beavan's. She had a very loud voice and few left her class illiterate. Playtime games were skipping, hopscotch and singing games.

PE was in the playground along with exercises, ball games and team games.

During the last year we were given gas masks as war was expected, and much noise was produced by the children by blowing hard out.

We were taken around one of the many cloth factories which would later give employment to many of the children. It was very noisy and smelt awful. We also went to Windsor Castle and came home part way on the Thames pleasure boat where we had tea. This was the last day out as the War came and stopped such things.

Our class had children from all sorts of backgrounds but we did not appear to notice except for one or two very poor boys who really did smell awful.

The heating was a big coke stove in one room which heated some radiators but we were used to cold houses and school.

It was a very academic school for all it was tiny, and Mr Daniel was keen for us to do well, although I felt that the boys were expected to do better than the girls.

I went to the Trowbridge High School afterwards with about five girls and five boys. It was a real struggle for my parents to pay the £1 per term High School fee as that was a lot of money then. We went to the High School for the interview after the exams. Mr Daniel said 'when you go and see the lady, look her straight in the face and answer the questions'. So, I got there and I thought, 'yes, I've got to look her straight in the face,' so I stared her in the eyes non-stop during the whole interview. I passed. I swear it was because I stared her right in the eyes.

THE 1940s

The evacuation of children from London was to mean major reorganisation in the senior school. On 31 May 1940, Newtown became Newtown Senior Boys Council School. The girls were taught in Trinity Church Hall and Bethesda Sunday School. Three weeks later the Hammersmith School of Building were evacuated to Trowbridge, and by the end of June there were 243 local boys and 66 evacuees in the school.

In 1940, Newtown was to become a Junior Mixed School, and new secondary schools were built on the Galley Farm site on Frome Road, the Nelson Haden Schools (Boys and Girls), for children over the age of eleven from the whole of Trowbridge.

The children, books and equipment from Trinity Junior School at Park Street were to come down to the Newtown building under their head, Mr Dyke-Meek, leaving the Park Street building empty. Throughout much of the Second World War it was to be used as an army barracks, particularly by American troops

Newtown School During the War
By Mrs Peggy Parsons (née Ladd)

I attended Newtown Junior School during the Second World War. We had to carry our gas-masks to school every day, which to me was a great nuisance. The first carrying case I had was black, and tubular and very ugly. Later I remember that I had a pigskin cover for the gas-mask which my father obtained from Beaven's Leather Factory in Holt.

When I was at Park Street we had a hilarious procedure we went through for our air raid precautions. My friend Joyce Burton had an Aunt who lived at the top of Newtown, and when our Air Raid Practice was carried out she and I had to run as fast as we could from Park Street to Auntie's house and crawl under her dining room table. By the time we returned to school, after enjoying some of Auntie's hospitality, our class had re-assembled and were getting on with their lessons. No one told us how long we should be so naturally we took as long as we could.

I can only remember four teachers. The Headmaster's name was Mr Meek and always seemed to be dressed in brown. Mr Daniel taught the top class and it was during his year that we took the 11-plus. He must have been a wonderful teacher as practically the whole class passed to go to the Grammar School and this was a class of sixty. Lots of names I remember to this day and often see my class mates around the town.

There was a lovely lady who was our form teacher, I think we were 2A. Her name was Miss Thomas and she and I got on very well together. Autograph books were all the rage that year and she wrote a little poem for me which goes as follows: Always be happy, never be sad./ That is my wish for Peggy Ladd. And for my friend Christine Cook she wrote: What shall I write in this little book/ All best wishes for Christine Cook. Not Shakespeare that's for sure, but it certainly impressed me.

Mrs Hayward was our sewing and knitting teacher. She must have despaired of me, as I remember taking about three terms to finish my iron holder. Not many people even know what an iron holder is. We had to use different colours on each side and each side had to be knitted in a different stitch. Mine was in light blue and dark blue wool. One side was in two plain, two purl stocking stitch, and horror of horrors the other side was in basket stitch. What a nightmare that was.

When I was lower down the school I was very envious of the top class, as when they had their singing lesson in the hall they sang a song which I think was called 'The River'. It had such a haunting tune, which I remember to this day. I also remember some of the words, and maybe someone could supply the ones I can't recall. '???????? the river/ Golden is the sand,/ it flows along for ever/ With trees on either hand. ????????? something from the foam/ ??????? the boats will soon come home.'

One strange thing I recall was the white painted line at the top end of the Newtown playground which we crossed at our peril. I think it was to keep us away from the railings near the pavement.

A story I recall was about the school dinners at Newtown Juniors. Our dinners were brought to the school in very large aluminium containers, and one day a certain teacher who was serving out the puddings found a PIN in the Rice Pudding. I can see her now carrying the pin along the corridor to the Headmaster's office.

My Memories of Newtown School
By Daphne White (née Hodge)

Looking back to the three years spent at Newtown School in the early forties my memories are mainly happy.

Classes were large in those days, made even larger by the influx of London evacuees. Fifty in a class was not unusual so there was not too much individual attention.

Discipline was strict and corporal punishment used at times. One master, Mr Daniel, a very fiery little Welshman, and a brilliant teacher, thought nothing of throwing the wooden blackboard cleaner at any miscreant, and indeed on occasion would throw a boy across the room if he incurred his wrath.

I remember suffering at the hands of our sewing teacher who used to thump us on the head with her thimble if our stitching failed to meet her standards.

This is the period of World War II and I have vivid memories of the air raid siren going off, and as I lived near the school, running with my sister to shelter under the kitchen table. [The children who lived near enough to the Trinity school to get home in a few minutes were allowed to go home in an air raid.] Once the whole school received a parcel from the USA. My sister remembers hers from Omaha, Nebraska containing Lux soap, toothpaste and sweets.

Morning lessons always began with mental arithmetic – about ten minutes of rapid fire questions. This was something that helped me in later years working in a bank and needing to add up long columns of figures in my head. Another memory I have is being asked to help the headmaster Mr Meek with filing paper work in his office for a few minutes a day. Would this happen today – I think not.

Of course, the big hurdle in those days was the 11-plus and I think records would show that Newtown produced excellent, above average results – perhaps the competition and large classes were no bad thing.

There were very few facilities for sport in those days as space was restricted as was equipment. Weather permitting visits were made to the open-air pool off Brown Street [where Tesco now stands]. As far as I can remember boys and girls went swimming at the same time.

Cars were rare in those days, children walked to school in small groups. My husband also went to Trinity Junior as it then was. His father was a farmer and he and his brothers walked from their house on the outskirts of Trowbridge near Upper Studley. Parents hardly ever needed to escort their children except while they were infants. Of course, traffic was very light – hardly any cars. Bicycles were most people's mode of transport, even groceries were delivered by cycle. Horses and carts figured quite large for delivering coal, parcels, etc. However, during the war years a large army presence in the town meant there was a certain amount of army vehicles. On leaving school at the end of the day pupils were crossed safely over Frome Road by their form teachers who made sure the road was clear.

School outings were virtually non-existent then, but if all this sounds as if we were missing out – not so. They were happy years in the forties. Incidentally I can still name forty pupils in my class – twenty-five girls and fifteen boys.

Trinity Infants and Newtown Juniors in the 1940s
By Avril Tadd

I commenced my schooling at the Trinity Infants School, Newtown in April 1941, I was taken to school on the first day by my father, and was accepted into the school by Miss Say. She had taught my father when he was very young, and was then known as Teacher Lily.

The school was built on two sides of a square, and according to my memory the corridor that ran in front of the classrooms on the inside of the square was open to the elements, but I might be wrong about this.

The Babies Class, as it was known, was situated on the extreme end of one side of the building, the teacher being either a Miss Davies who became Mrs Jones, or a Miss Jones who became Mrs Davies. Apart from the usual tables and chairs in the room there were toys, the only ones I remember are the sand pit and the dolls house that had electricity, a great novelty as we did not have electricity at home, also it was large enough to be able to walk inside it.

I then moved to the next class, the teacher was Miss Say, who lived in Park Street with her sister. My main memories of this class is that Miss Say taught us singing games, i.e. Old MacDonald Had A Farm, The Farmer Wants A

Wife and there were others. My feeling now is that Miss Say was still teaching because it was War Time.

The next move was to the class taught by Miss Cook, who lived in Dursley Road and whose brother invented iridescent paint. Miss Cook used to decorate her class by a frieze made by herself from brown paper with cut outs of various objects, usually flowers, glued on. This frieze stretched all the way around three sides of the room and was about 15–18" deep, she used to impress on us the fact that it took her at least a week to make.

Of the other teachers one was called Miss Thomas, another Mrs York (who lived in Bradford Road) and there was one more whose name I cannot remember. The headmistress was Miss Blanchard who lived with her sister in Newtown quite close to the school.

There was a little cloakroom, situated at the junction of the two wings, it had a row of small low wash basins, but I don't remember leaving my coat there and neither do I remember if the toilets were inside or outside. I never remember going outside for Gym, we used to stand next to our desks and do exercises there. There was a large climbing frame on the large grass area next to the tarmac playground.

On one occasion we all had to go to the Newtown Junior School to be immunised against diphtheria, when our mothers were requested to accompany us, there were many tears.

Newtown Junior School

In Newtown Junior School there was a separate large playground, covered with tarmac, for girls and one for boys, with a brick wall around the outside and a separating brick wall down through the middle. We also had separate cloakrooms for boys and girls where we left our coats, there were also wash basins there. The toilets were outside across the playground, two for girls on one side and two for boys on the other. As you look at Newtown School from Newtown, the girls entered on the right and the boys on the left. There was also a grassy garden that ran, on the girls side, from Newtown down towards the railway line and then at right angles along the bottom of the playgrounds, we were very rarely allowed in there and then only under supervision.

During our playtime we engaged in singing games in the playground such as Hunt the Fox, The Good Ship Sails on the Allee, Allee Oh, etc., and other games which I have now forgotten.

Here again, I don't remember having Gym outside, but I expect we did, as we were all divided into different teams, red, blue, green and yellow and wore the appropriate coloured braid over our shoulders. We certainly did exercises standing next to our desks, as part of the main Hall was used as a classroom. At Newtown School I remember being introduced to English Folk Dancing, but where we did this I cannot remember.

I don't remember the name of the first teacher there, but the classroom was situated on the right-hand side overlooking the playground.

The next teacher was Mrs Rodway, who taught us Folk Dancing. Here again we did exercises beside our desks. We learnt our mathematics tables by rote, if individually we could recite any table correctly on the day we learnt it – we could go home early. While in Mrs Rodway's class I suffered with a Grumbling Appendix and was away from school from about March until July when my appendix was removed, during the whole of that time Mrs Rodway sent home work for me, my father used to collect and deliver this work.

I then moved on to Mrs Hayward's class, another lady who was still only teaching because of War Time. I learnt the meaning of incentive here, Mrs Hayward on a Friday morning had a lesson called Mental Arithmetic, she read out twenty questions and if you had them all correct she gave you a penny. It was during this year that we started to have swimming lessons, in unheated water at the Trowbridge Swimming Pool in Brown Street, we used to walk there in a crocodile.

The last class I was in was situated in the Hall, taken by a Miss Leroy, she left to be a missionary part way through the year and we then had a Mr Boulting and a Mr Matthew Wray jointly. This was the time when members of the Armed Forces were returning to civilian occupation. During this year the weather was very cold and we were allowed to wear our coats for our lessons in the Hall, I remember my grandmother knitted me a pair of fingerless mittens.

There were other teachers, but I only remember the names of two, a Miss Beaven who became a G.I. Bride and Mrs Maslen. Mr Dyke-Meek, who lived in Trowbridge Road, Bradford on Avon, was headmaster for the whole of the time I was at Newtown Junior School.

At the back of the school, facing the playground and between two protruding classrooms. were two other rooms, one the headmaster's room and the other the kitchen which the teachers used as a staff room. Meals were not cooked at the school, these were all cooked at the Central Kitchens located in Holt, and were delivered daily by road, the part of the Hall not used as a classroom then became the dining room. The infants who lived too far away to be able to go home for luncheon came to the Junior school for their meal.

We used to have periodic visits from the School Nurse, when screens were erected in the Hall and we used to file in to see her one by one, I remember she was always called 'The Nit Lady'.

At the end of my time at Newtown Junior School we received Fancy Gift Wrapped Presents from the children of America, I had never seen fancy wrapping paper before. Among the items I received was a long string of pink beads that I wore for many years (I think I gave it to the Museum). Insufficient parcels were delivered to the school for all the pupils to have one each, so the staff unwrapped all of the parcels and divided them between all of us.

Taking the 11-Plus
By Maureen Duffy

This contribution comes from Maureen Duffy's semi-autobiographical novel *That's how it was*, first published in 1962, which is set in the town of Wortbridge. Maureen Duffy was evacuated to Trowbridge in the war and took her 11-plus examination at Newtown. The Mr Evans mentioned is undoubtedly based on the redoubtable Mr Daniel. The extract from *That's how it was* is reprinted by permission of Virago Press.

'If only it weren't so cold it would be easier.' Or would it have been? I'm not so sure. I remember too many exams taken in broiling heat so you dripped mingled sweat and ink from your pen and your head buzzed fly-like at the window of memory. But then there was that other horrible time when we all sniffed and snivelled and blew our snotty noses and coughed over our papers til every word must have been crawling with minute life, and worst of all I'd forgotten my handkerchief, only by then they were nose-rags, old sheets torn up and hemmed, bits of shirt tail and faded summer dresses split under the arms, the tops that is, the skirts were remade into blouses. My mother had a splendid method of boiling the dressing out of flour-bags and hemming them up, and lovely and soft to a sore nose they were too, only this day I hadn't got a thing, not a scrap of rag and my nose kept running, sitting in the chilly, stuffy room. But no one must know. How terrible to be seen with a runny nose. I cuffed it craftily, then, in desperation, I blotted it with my new square of pink examination blotting paper. I felt a miserable slum kid, though Mavis Cooper, the doctor's daughter, picked hers and worse. The whole idea made me retch; hastily I fixed my mind on the paper itself – anything was better than that.

This time it was cold and damp, grey and the lights were on. At ten o'clock we would pick up our pencils and start. It was two minutes to. On the far side of the hall the headmaster was still giving out papers. There were three to do, intelligence, English, arithmetic. This was the intelligence. 'If Cousin Gilly can do it,' I thought, 'so can I.'

The second hand swung through the last minute.

'Pick up your pencils and begin.'

I read the instructions very carefully, sure that I shouldn't be able to write at all. Time was important. If you didn't finish they couldn't give you marks for what you hadn't done. Mr Evans had explained that again and again. All my class were there and lots of strange boys and girls from schools not big enough to be a centre.

'You're young,' my mother had said. 'Don't worry. If you don't pass you can try again next year.' But that wasn't it. If I didn't pass I was stupid. There'd be nothing for me. I couldn't go to sea, round the world, cross the desert on a camel like my current hero Lawrence of Arabia – I sat in trees, on ant-hills, for what seemed hours on end, while I was stung or got hideous cramp, so I could be another blue-eyed Arab. I dressed in a sheet and painted my skin with my brown water-colour paint like Kim but I was just a girl and life offered only things I despised, houses, children, security, housework. I had to pass. I had to. I had to be different. There must be more to life than this or there wasn't any point in being born. And there had to be a point for her sake.

I began the questions.

'If you can't do one, leave it and go on to the next. Don't waste time,' Mr Evans sang and roared in my head.

'*Branch* is to *tree* as *arm* is to: head, bone, body, leg.'

I underlined *body* and went on.

With ten minutes to spare I came to the end of eighty-nine questions and sat back, just time to look them all through to see if I'd made a mistake. Then I saw the boy in front looking at the back page. I hadn't thought to turn over. It seemed so logical to end at the bottom on the second inside page. The boy turned back to the beginning and began to go all through. Terrified I turned over. There were eleven more questions and only nine minutes to go. Of course, how stupid, I knew there were a hundred questions, I knew, I knew. Shakily I began on them, the hardest, kept til last. I finished with a minute to spare. There was no time to look through the rest. The headmaster called time, the papers were gathered, somehow, we got up and went silently to the milk table. The milk had been warmed against the radiators and tasted slightly sour but it was probably the taste of fear. My legs felt weak and thin as if I had been in bed for a fortnight. Two more papers to go.

When I got to the front gate I held it right back against the fence and shot off as I let it go. If I could get to the bend in the lane before it crashed to it would be alright, good luck. I ran as if I would die; I made it.

[Ed. – Maureen Duffy passed her 11-plus and went to the Girls High School.]

Fifty Years on
By David Crook

School began in September 1944 with a visit to Miss Blanchard's Office. This was up a flight of stairs in the Trinity Infant School and I was accompanied by my mother.

My next visit to this office occurred some months later. We had been told that white lines were to be painted on the playground and we were ordered to stay away from them. A couple of hours in the life of a five-year-old is a long time and my forgetfulness caused Miss Blanchard to use the ruler on each of my hands. I think she must have been very gentle though, because the ruler did not hurt much. Sometime after this one of the local policemen came and spoke to the assembled infants on road safety. In particular he spent some time teaching us how to cross the road without being hurt.

Once again, my stupidity made me forget these lessons and only a few days later I had my left foot run over by the back wheel of a car at the junction of Park Street and Frome Road. By the time I arrived at the Infants my foot was badly swollen and my friend John Workman was helping me walk. I had a great fear of the police at this time and I made my colleagues promise not to tell what had happened, but to say only that I had tripped over. To a man they supported my lie. The teachers all came to look at my foot and the morning passed in pain. John Workman again helped me home for dinner. We were so late arriving our mothers were very worried. I told my lie again to my mother, but this time John told his mother the truth. She, of course, came to our door and my deception was exposed. The policeman came to our house and I imagined I was going to prison for telling such untruths. I wondered what the fuss was about when they kept saying they would find the car driver, when I knew it was my fault for not crossing the road properly and I was glad they never found him.

These events were from my time in the reception class and my next school year was to be with Miss Say. This lady was a legend amongst the children for being a disciplinarian. I remember a few days in her class, but then I was ill for some time and missed the majority of the school year. Mrs Cook was next and I was very happy in her class, then likewise in Mrs Miller's class and on to Mrs Hayward.

I believe Mrs Hayward had been teaching at the school for many years and she was an excellent teacher, keeping us in order and making us work and learn. One day towards the end of the academic year September 1948–July 1949 she propped open the classroom door and kept running out. We never saw this kind lady again. She had been more than a teacher to us and it was with sadness that we heard of her death.

The supply teacher who was Mrs Hayward's replacement was a man who did not understand children. He would scream and shout all the time and we were terrified. He set me to write 500 lines for talking. This was asking the impossible. A page of our exercise book had twenty lines on and I soon realised he was ordering me to fill a book with writing as a punishment. I had just started this task when one of the children was sick in class. This creature put sawdust on the mess and said to me that he would let me off the punishment if I filled a bucket and emptied it in the school garden. So, I never completed the 500 lines, but I nourished contempt in my heart for this man.

A host of other memories, crowd my mind. The junior playground was divided by a brick wall, boys on one side, girls on the other. The seasons rang the changes in the playground, five stones, conkers, gang warfare came and went, along with various games of touch. Assemblies, singing 'I vow to thee my country', etc., chanting the times tables every day, handwriting practice from inkwells filled with blotting paper using scratchy pen nibs, school dinners where I tried to sit next to Gloria Purbrick because she used to pass some of her food on, the occasional lesson in the playground of 'drill' and learning to swim a width at Trowbridge Swimming Pool, all combined with the memories of chalk, blackboards and learning.

I finally left the school in July 1950, which coincided with the departure of the Headteacher, Mr Meek. Six years of my life were spent at Newtown. Half a century has passed, and the education scene is transformed, but the basic truths which Newtown taught remain the same.

Memories of Trinity and Newtown at the End of the War
By Christine Shaw (née Rodway)

I started School near the end of the war. I have an impression of Trinity Infants' School being one long corridor full of windows criss-crossed with brown sticky paper. We lined up in this corridor to pay our dinner money 2s-6d. 2s-1d for dinners and 5d for milk. We had to practise what to do if there should be an air-raid. We used to take little boards to sit on in the cloakroom.

One Christmas the school received parcels from the USA, there were things like ribbons and hair slides and I had a little brooch made out of a walnut shell. It was a little face with yellow plaits.

We used to have our gas masks regularly inspected. Mine was a Mickey Mouse one. I thought my brother was important because he had one like the grown-ups. It was a strange feeling putting the mask over my face. I did not like it at all. We also always wore identity discs with our name and address on.

We seemed to have regular efforts to save for Victory. I think there must have been special National Savings weeks. We used to take money for National Savings Stamps.

I do not remember using much paper in the Infants' School. We always wrote on little blackboards and we always had a little square rubber made out of a type of felt material.

By this time my mother [Mrs Bessie Rodway - Ed.] was sometimes teaching at Newtown. The infants had to go to the Junior School for their dinner. To a small infant the Junior School seemed to be packed with big children, there were classes at both ends of the School Hall. The dinners came in big containers. There always seemed to be an awful lot of beetroot. I did not like the way it made the potato pink.

I was still an infant when the end of the war came. The thing that most impressed me was that Miss Blanchard came into the classroom and said that we could have biscuits with our milk. The school must have had quite a supply of biscuits in case children could not go home because of air raids. They lasted for ages.

We learnt the National Anthem at school for the Victory Services, all the verses. We also learnt 'O God Our Help in Ages Past' but I did not understand the words. I could not work out why the 'suns' went away.

I was in the infant playground looking at the trains go by when we saw a train with bananas written on one of the goods waggons. Everyone went wild, we did not know what bananas were but we thought they must be nice.

I was at Newtown School from 11-9-46 to 1949. In those days the first year junior class was in the Infants' School. Our teacher was Miss Cook. When we were ready to go to the Junior School we were given a talk by Miss Blanchard, the infant headmistress about being grown up and sensible. As the top infant classroom windows overlooked the junior playground she said she would haul us back if she saw us misbehaving. Newtown, the 'big school', was fairly familiar to us as we went there for school dinners.

Mr Meek was the headmaster of Newtown in my day. I started in 2A with Mrs Alpe in the small room with a fireplace. The desks were the old wood and iron ones joined together in twos with fold-up seats. Mrs Miller took the class next door. Part way through the year Mrs Alpe left and my mother took the class.

When I first started Newtown there were two classes in the hall, one at each end. The class nearest the road was taken by Mrs Learoy, but I do not think that was for very long. I cannot think who took the class at the clock end, but that was there for some time as the children who brought sandwiches for dinner ate their dinner there.

As far as I can remember, Miss Thomas took 3A, Mrs Beavan and Mrs Maslin took the classes on the other side of the hall and Miss Bevan took 4A. Miss Beavan married an American and went to Philadelphia. She sent the school some sweets as there was, of course, still sweet rationing in England. Every pupil had a wrapped sweet. I think Miss Beavan's place was taken by Mr Boulding and Mrs Sparkes and Mr Ewing came at some time, but I cannot remember exactly when.

I was very happy at Newtown School. The thing I loved best was the garden, not that I went in it very much, but the boys had gardening lessons when we had needlework. I would have loved to have had gardening lessons. There was a lovely lawn and flower border, but the rest was divided into plots, no doubt for the war effort. I remember the boys growing carrots, lettuces and radishes and I think beans. We planted plenty of beans and peas in jars with pink blotting paper, so they were probably what ended up in the garden. When we were in 4A we were doing some plays, and were allowed to practise in the garden at the end nearest the Infants' School This was a beautiful part of the garden with a lawn and a herbaceous border down one side.

I can still remember most of the things I learned at Newtown. The teaching must have been very thorough and we had a good grounding in all subjects. We learned English grammar far more thoroughly than my children did. We did English exercises every day from *Commonsense English*. There were poems in those books as well, some by Rose Fyleman and William Blake. I can still recite them. There were also quite a few passages and fables for comprehension. We had some geography books called *Columbus Regional Geographies* all about people from other lands and in later ones about different areas of England and their industries. We learned a lot about coal mining in 4A and the woollen industry, especially relating to Trowbridge.

There was a huge map of Trowbridge on the wall outside Mr Meeks's room. How different Trowbridge was then; the population was 12,000 and it did not seem to change much.

In the corridor behind the hall, the PE equipment was stored. There were a lot of oval mats made of a sort of coconut matting. These probably dated from before the war as they were somewhat the worse for wear. We used these for various activities in the playground.

History and nature study were my favourite lessons. Throughout the junior classes we learned about English history from the Romans to the 20th century. It was a very good background to the history I learned later, as I have always been able to relate events to their historical time scale. At the back of our history books there was a good time chart and that must have been impressed on my mind.

We always had interesting nature tables in the classrooms. I loved it when it was my turn to look after the nature table. I remember some very good radio nature lessons with very colourful pamphlets to go with them.

The classes at Newtown in my day were very large, but we seemed to be able to do interesting things – potato cuts, paste painting – and I think we did some lino cuts and scrapboard pictures in 4A.

We learned to knit socks in needlework, in pink or blue rather stringy wool. We made them with a partner, but unfortunately my partner and I did not knit at the same tension and one sock was quite large and the other small. I cannot think what happened about that. I made a rabbit pincushion out of brown hessian with blanket stitch round the edges and a belt out of brown felt with oranges and lemons on it. I was not very good at sewing then so making an apron was quite a trial.

Daily assemblies were held in the hall. The hymns were written on big sheets. At Christmas there was a Schools' Carol Festival so we learned a wide selection of carols. I went one year to Trinity Church and once to Emmanuel Church. Mr Oakshott conducted it.

We went swimming when we were in the top junior classes to the swimming pool at the bottom of the park. It was not heated in those days and the water was often very cold. Mr Toombs was in charge. I learned to swim just before I went to the High School. We were allowed to buy a 2d cup of hot lemon if we got dressed in time

Country dancing was very popular in my junior school days. I think we had classes after school. There was a country dance festival in Devizes and I was very excited about going, but unfortunately, I got measles so was unable to go.

The 11-plus examination was the big hurdle for the top juniors. We all sat at desks in the hall for the exam. It was quite an ordeal, but at least we learned a lot in preparation for it and it was a good grounding for the future. A large proportion of children got to the High Schools from Newtown.

School dinners will always be a lasting memory. They came from Holt and varied in their standard and content. On the whole they were quite good, but there seemed to be an awful lot of smash-type of potato and brown cabbage. There were some nice puddings, jam tart and treacle pudding, but I have never been able to eat macaroni, semolina or sage with any enthusiasm as I had such a lot of school dinners. At least once the dinners did not arrive and Mr Meek sent out for bread and we had sandwiches.

The dinner playtime seemed to be quite long. Playground games went in crazes. One time it might be marbles (we used to roll them into holes on the piece of playground near the outside toilets) or making bracelets and necklaces out of a kind of plastic thread. We would have a thicker piece as the base and we used to weave other coloured strands over it. Necklaces could be made from this thread by knitting a few stitches and twisting them.

There was quite a ritual with ball games. We bounced balls against the playground wall. There were rhymes – 'Touch your knee, touch your toe, dap the ball and over she goes.' The same thing applied to skipping games, some which we played with a large rope and rhymes such as 'I'm a Girl guide dressed in blue' and various others when as many people as possible tried to skip together. It was very hard getting in and out. There were individual skipping rhymes as well when we did bumps, side skips and crosses. Then there were the dipping rituals to see who was 'on it'.

Inky pinky ponky, daddy bought a donkey,

Donkey died, daddy cried, inky pinky ponky.

We often played charades at dinner time and 'Queenie, Queenie, who's got the ball?' and 'Please Jack, may I cross the water?' We all joined the Ovaltinies at one stage and we had a book which we had to fill in. We were supposed to do a chivalrous deed for one page and then you could fill in a coat of arms, but I did not have a clue what chivalry was. We also all read Enid Blyton's *Sunny Stories* and we enjoyed them very much. I took the *Children's Newspaper* for a time and we also filled in the *I Spy* books from Big Chief I Spy of the *News Chronicle*.

There were no inside toilets at Newtown in my day and the outside ones used to freeze. 1947 was a particularly hard winter so it must have caused a great many problems for the caretaker.

Sweets were rationed throughout my junior school years, but there was a craze for eating Ovaltine tablets and liquorice sticks.

Just after the war, Newtown School was not full of luxuries, but we managed to enjoy our school life and get a great deal out of it which has stood me in good stead for the rest of my life.

Trinity Infants, Park Street and Newtown Junior –
Some Recollections from Fifty Years Ago
By John Austin

As I was born in 1940 I imagine that I began at the Infants' School sometime in 1945. My first day was memorable for being praised by Miss Jones for my drawing of an elephant and for her later dressing me in a pair of voluminous, dusty, green knickers as I had wet myself, being too shy a little boy to ask to be taken to the lav. Miss Blanchard, who ruled over us from somewhere up the stairs, seemed to combine a severe sternness with glimpses of kindness. Miss Hall, who replaced her during my time, was less remote and consequently less awesome.

In the second class we were taught for a time by Miss Say, a white-haired disciplinarian who had probably been brought out of retirement to help out in time of need. She taught us how to lay a fire, bringing in newspaper, kindling wood and coal and setting up the demonstration in the seat of her high teacher's chair. No match was struck! In that great long room, we learned our numbers from cards and in my mind's eye I still visualise single digits as sets of dots, with a 7 for example consisting of five symmetrically arranged dots above the line and two more below. Music was a continuing disappointment for me, ever desperately wishing for the drum but invariably being allocated the boring triangle. A visit by Father Christmas was rather a shock as I had thought that he only came on Christmas Eve, at home, at night – when I was safely asleep.

A little later, maybe with another Ms Jones, poor Terry owned up to stealing by answering 'Where is Averil's coat?' with 'On my bed at home Miss'. He was made to strip off his jumper and shirt and stood shivering in the corner for a while, learning how Averil had suffered having to go home in the cold with no coat. There were several children from very poor families, some of them living in the Nissan huts near the Black Horse on the huge, largely redundant barracks, where, incidentally, I inadvertently attended a briefing of GIs about to leave for the invasion of France, but that is another story. One bright sunny day we were given chocolate, presumably as a belated celebration of the ending of hostilities.

In the unsegregated playground we chose to play in separate sexes and suffered from spreethed legs in the winter cold. Why didn't we all wear long trousers? Us boys mainly played galloping, either singly, slapping our horse bottoms with one hand and pumping imaginary reins with the other, or else in pairs, arms linked behind our backs and feet synchronised, going like the wind. My partner and I once bashed into Sheila Barker, who I loved very dearly then and on through Junior School (sorry Mrs Lerwell), and we were chastised verbally for being too rough. Beyond the playground proper, to the left, I remember a secluded place, with railings, from where we could watch and wave to the trains.

A bit older and 'round the corner' we had craft classes when we tried to make exciting things from promising materials like cotton reels and cardboard boxes but were generally frustrated by blunt scissors that made one's fingers sore with the effort and very inadequate glue. Nothing more academic comes to mind than drawing and colouring in repetitive patterns, lots of orange in mine.

In what seemed no time at all we were off to Park Street and Miss Maslen, Miss Wickham and Mrs Rodway and high windows you couldn't see out of, but with the sills adorned with the flowers we were encouraged to bring in, arranged in painted jam jars, one of them a ghastly pink with blue spots. There was more drawing (Mrs Rodway tells me all these years later that I was good at perspective, but not too good at spelling, now I'm no good at either) and lots of singing, one song going something like 'The first shot he missed, the second one he kissed – down in the derry derry down oh'.

Eventually, when I was eight I suppose, up to the big school and what should have been Miss Thomas's class. However, we had for a while Mr Ferguson who wore a blue jumper and a fierce temper to match his red hair. We spent a while each day lying on oval rush mats that had a peculiar but pleasant smell. In the next class I remember a visitor (HMI?) noisily decrying Enid Blyton to Mr Napthene. In fact, he read us good literature like *Three Men in a Boat* when he cried with laughter, unable for ages to conclude the passage where George and Harris throw each other out of bed.

At about this time I began to attend 'remedial' classes which included exercises like 'caterpillars crawling' which involved scrunching up one's (removed) sock with one's toes, which I was good at, and several other exercises for inadequate feet which were less enjoyable. My feet are still rather shapeless despite the remedials and the best efforts of Cliff and Tom Taylor who built up the heels of my shoes at Tuckers (why not Taylors?) in Fore Street.

Another disaster at this time was my taking up the violin. I am now feeling muddled and it may be that 'caterpillars crawling' was an excruciating exercise twixt cat gut and horse hair. The best memory of the violin episode, which dragged on to the High School, was of seeing some very interesting bits of anatomy down the front of the dress of the peripatetic music teacher as she knelt before me trying to will a sweeter sound from my instrument. Music figured more pleasantly when the new head master (Mr Warburton replacing Mr Dyke-Meek) installed loudspeakers in the hall so that we could enter assembly to the stirring sounds of the 'Trumpet Voluntary' and other uplifting pieces. He also introduced proper cricket, with wickets marked out in the boys' playground, stumps set in wooden blocks, proper sprung bats and rubber covered composition balls. In front of the crease a white oblong showed where the bowler should try to pitch on a length. The soccer team was also freshly kitted out in shirts of maroon and white quarters with Pat Andrews in goal in a green roll neck jumper, a la Bert Vince, the Trowbridge Town keeper.

In Pop Boulding's class we began to approach adolescence and Maggie and Anne began to look a bit bumpy under their jumpers. Brian Withers made Cliff Skinner 'spuggle' his milk and he was sent out, only to keep reappearing, passing and repassing the glass panelled door and grinning in at us. Eventually Pop twigged what was going on and rushed out to confront our entertainer to be deflated to find that Cliff was about legitimate business, having been commandeered by the head to some repetitive task.

Cliff was one of several boys who could defy the laws of biology and physics by 'going over' the open urinal wall into the lane leading to the Infants'. Oddly this antisocial behaviour never seemed to be reported and along with fights and a bit of bullying was either tolerated or unknown to the staff who hardly ever appeared in the playground at break.

A great pleasure of the playground, apart from the traditional marbles, conkers, five stones and fighting was miniature cricket. Some boys made wonderful bats, adorned with paint and black tape. Wickets were chalked against a wall but otherwise the laws were more or less standard although the game was played kneeling or at the crouch. The playground characters were the really big boys like Cliff, Colin Kettlety and Mick Paviour and the most amazingly athletic Bob Wyatt always accompanied by his best friend Arthur Bancroft. Now and then exotica turned up from far off lands like Cornwall and the USA, sporting strange accents and basketball boots. In our class the cleverest person was Nancy Holdroyd, a newcomer. Among the locals Cliff was one of the ablest, with wonderfully neat and attractive handwriting.

Us boys did gardening and to our surprise the most proficient was John 'Wurzzle' Golledge who dug a neat and nifty spit even though he hated all other outdoor pursuits. When Pop wasn't around, seeing Miss Thomas no doubt, who, to our amazement he married, we threw small hard apples at each other and at passing trains until there was a row. After gardening we had to clean and oil all the tools and replace them in the shed in the playground. Brian Withers discovered that rude noises could be made by blowing down the spout of a watering can and he and Pat Andrews blew up a storm by giving a rendition through the ventilator into the fierce Mr Sparkes' classroom.

The only out of school event, apart from sports fixtures was a train excursion with some parents and staff to Windsor Castle, followed by a river trip to Runnymede. The train left from the far platform, the flags in St George's Chapel were gossamer thin and torn and Dave Culverhouse lost his cap and nearly his head when he stood up when passing under a low bridge over the Thames.

When I had to attend the clinic I was sent on the long trudge to The Halve in the care of an older boy, Vivian Warburton I think. The dentist there was Mr Young whose daughter Marion was in our class and who made a big thing out of her Jewish faith.

From the shops in Newtown we bought white and yellow 'sherbert', short lengths of wood, both thick and thin, which we chewed till our jaws ached to extract the delicious yellow sap, leaving a bundle of frayed white fibres. Ice lollies came on the scene at Hancocks; shop-made conical efforts whose pale pastel shades vanished with the first few sucks, to leave a still novel blob of ice on a stick. Hardly anyone had refrigerators in those days, I knew of only one in Bradley Road where I lived and from where I cycled to school from about the age of nine with very little traffic to worry about.

Some of these memories are, I am sure, accurate recollections of experiences at the three schools, we were not at all aware of whether Park Street belonged to the Infants or the Junior or whether it was independent. Some images are undoubtedly incorrect, being the product of a vivid imagination allied to vague half remembered impressions of a way of life that is certainly gone for ever. Much will have improved for the better but do they still play miniature cricket, and if not would they like to be shown? I hope so.

Trinity and Newtown in the late 1940s and early 1950s
By Brian Withers

I guess my memories of Newtown started when one sunny afternoon in the summer of 1945 I was dressed up smartly by Mum and walked from Holbrook Lane to what I suppose was a kind of interview with Miss Blanchard. The content of what was asked of me has gone and all I can remember is the floor of her room strewn with sit-in toy trains and trolleys. To all accounts by the look on Mum's face all had gone well and I was in, and to start my education process at the beginning of the new term in September. The Second World War had just come to an end. We were indeed entering a new era!!

The first day of school finally came round. This was to be my first break from the apron strings but I think it hurt Mum more than me. My sister, Diane, was barely a year old and she was bundled into the pram and off we set around The Croft, along Bradley Road, down Frome Road to the Ship Inn and cross the road there and so on to the halls of learning. From day one I convinced Mum that her escort was not needed in the future but she had befriended some woman who lived at the junction of Bradley and Frome Road to keep an eye on me. I think I saw her once and that was it.

So, this was Infants' School. Class I or whatever it was called was situated on the north wing of the building and within the room was what appeared to be a huge play house for the purpose of playing, I gather. I do not recall the teacher's name but for a considerable time, the education process appeared to be hands up. 'Hands up who can read what is on the blackboard. Hands up who knows what time it is. Hands up who wants another bottle of milk. Hands up who wants to go to the lavatory!!'

There were two rituals which interrupted the day's progress of learning. At 11 a.m. it was milk time. Thanks probably to Clem Attlee's Government all children of school age were entitled to a one third pint bottle of milk per school day. One problem. I hated milk. I still hate milk. What made it worse was that with winter now approaching, the bottles were stacked on the classroom radiators to warm the milk. To this day, the thought of the warming milk still churns my stomach. By mid-afternoon we were forced to take a rest. Was this for us or the teachers? Oval multi-coloured rush mats were gathered from a corner of the class room by each of us and we were made to lie on them for this rest. Time seemed endless. How boring. What was it all for? I didn't have a rest at home. Why the devil did I need one here?

Christmas was now approaching and from my point of view almost everything stopped for the preparation, with every pupil surrounded with coloured paper, paste and scissors making stars and crowns. The best in the class had silver and gold paper to make their crowns. I had plain blue paper to which I was already consoling myself that at the very best I was just average, but at least we were all in the choir. There followed practice upon practice of singing carols and the inevitable Nativity Play. I think I played Shepherd No.5 dressed in an old bedroom curtain found discarded in our garden shed. Eventually the big day arrived which culminated in a visit from no other than Father Christmas. I still believed in Father Christmas and had convinced Mum and Dad that this one was the real one and that the one portrayed by 'Donkey' Woods at Fear Hills was a phony. However, this 'real' one had a striking similar appearance and voice of our next door neighbour, George Mattock from the Education Dept. at County Hall. He was also a school governor.

I spent two years in the Infants but how we progressed classwise, now eludes me. All I know is that I sat in three different classrooms. I cannot recall the names of the first two teachers but the first one was a short lady with blonde curly hair and a kindly disposition.

The second one was, I believe, a temporary teacher from USA. I think this was the first time I ever had a crush on anyone. She was very good looking and very sweet with it. I had a new interest in school!! The third class, Miss Wickham was the teacher. There was another class above me presided over by Miss Cook. We were all more or less the same age and the penny then dropped. I was in the B Class. Learning of the 3 R's continued and we were now learning to do joined up writing in ink. With that came the appointment of the ink monitor whose duty it was to ensure that everyone's inkwell was topped up by some ink solution poured from an enamel teapot. Most of us by this time could read simple story books, write reasonably well, albeit smudges and numerous blots, and had conquered the mysteries of elementary arithmetic. Now two periods a week were introduced, band and drama. The band session was basically purely percussion. Why was I always given the triangle? My interest faded rapidly. With drama, I also took a back seat as I recall an enactment in the classroom of *The Sleeping Beauty*. Prince Charming (Billy Forbes) hacked his way through imaginary twines, briars and undergrowth to reach and awaken the Sleeping Beauty (Jennifer Rogers) lying comatose across two desks!! And we all yelled out, 'And he awoke Briar Rosebud with a kiss.' Did he? I just can't remember.

I only entered Miss Cook's class once and that was for punishment. I was made to stand for what appeared to be all afternoon, with my face towards the blackboard with my hands on my head. I had caused two teeth to be released from Terry Bishop's gums. What the argument had been about, I don't know. Perhaps Terry can, as he had the opportunity to gloat as I did penance. The incident still disturbs me as I was not, and never had been a belligerent soul.

We now had our foundation and after the long summer holiday, we would move to the Big School, Newtown Junior.

To a seven-year-old in those days, Newtown Junior School building appeared massive, especially from the interior. Before my first day there, I think I had only been inside one larger building and that was the Town Hall on a couple of occasions when I had accompanied Dad to pay the rates.

To my surprise, I was put into 2A, Mrs Rodway's class. New subjects were introduced like Geography and History. I liked these subjects and it is the only time that the word 'Excellent' ever appeared on any of my school reports in reference to these two subjects only. The school year being divided into three terms, these would be our first school reports at the end of each term. This year we had three different teachers for each term. Firstly Mrs Rodway, then Mr Conroy (he was temporary) and finally Ms Hillman. They all reported on me with monotony with the exception as mentioned, viz: A Plodder, Could do better, Must try harder next term. Ah, but I did get Good for attendance and believe it or not, Good for conduct!!

One subject which appeared to consume hours was arithmetic in the form of Bills, e.g.: Four and a quarter yards of calico at three shillings and sixpence farthing a yard plus about seven other items at similar ridiculous quantities and price and all added up. I guess it kept our heads oiled but how lucky are today's pupils when everything is metricated. We must have wasted two years of productive mathematics to cater for this pedantic slog.

Reading and writing now progressed into the inspirational subject of the likes of grammar, comprehension and poetry, all contained within the text book *The Common Sense English Course*. I could have made a bonfire out of the forty odd copies distributed to the class. However, I 'plodded' on.

We now started to bring items to and from school. Things like pencil boxes, the wooden swivel type with a sliding top into which nothing standard would fit. The thing weighed a ton and would only hold a few pencils and you even had to cut a normal rubber in half to fit it into the darned hole provided. Thus, for so-called art, I had an HB, red, blue, yellow and green pencils and that was my lot. Maureen Hayward who sat behind me had it all worked out. She had a cloth roll into which slotted every conceivable coloured pencil. She used to boss me about and would she lend me her mauve pencil, would she hell. Sorry Maureen, I had to get you back one day!!

We did not see too much of Mr Meek the headmaster except at morning assembly or when there were special announcements, but his presence was always evident. I remember him most for his teasing of Molly Fuller who was I believe his pet monitor. For morning assembly, we would line up by classes in the playground and then march into main hall. We then said a few prayers and sung a hymn. We had no hymn books and we followed the words from large cards held up by boys from 3B standing on chairs.

Sport was not very much in evidence at this time. We must have had some kind of Sports Day but my memory is blank on this one. Our recreation was in the playground. Tag and touch games were prominent and then there were the phases of marbles, five stones and in the autumn, conkers of course. No bakers or picklers permitted. Skirmishes and fights broke out occasionally and usually lasted only a minute or so until one of the parties succumbed before a teacher came to break it up. One of the best fights was between Arthur Rogers and Peter York, both I believe in 4B at the time. What it was all about is probably unknown history. The consensus of opinion was that Yorky won, but both survived.

My first year had been completed. Number in Class 44: Position 37. At least there were seven others worse than me!! So, I progressed to Mr Napthene's class, 3A. To me this was to be a non-event year. Arithmetic became harder, Common Sense English was still with us and I still plodded on. Thank heavens still for History and Geography which prevented me from becoming a total non-person in the academic field. On top of all this I was still a shy little boy lacking a lot of self-confidence. By this time, I had joined the Cubs at North

Bradley which gave me another interest. I enjoyed the Cubs and knew I was a good one too. It would take over a year before I would come out of my shell. This reminds me of another event which has passed into history. We celebrated 'Empire Day'. If we belonged to any youth organisation, e.g.: Cubs, Brownies, Boys' Brigade, etc., we would wear our uniforms to school. This gave me a chance to show off my one star and proficiency badges and this was only the beginning.

Time was starting to move at a quicker tempo now and before I knew it, summer holidays were with us again. My report from Mr Napthene read almost word for word as the previous year. Nevertheless, my position in class had been maintained and next term I would be admitted to 4A, Mr Boulding's class and prepare for the 11-plus examination.

This is when I really started to enjoy school with yet another bonus. We were at this age allowed to cycle to school. My bicycle was a second-hand Rudge Whitworth that Dad had managed to pick up from some source. He had modified it with bits obtained from Wilfy Jones' bike repair yard, which was situated behind Earl's shoe repair shop in Newtown at the bottom of Gloucester Road. To cycle to and from school enabled me to have a longer time for dinner. I had always walked home for dinner except for a short while when I tried school meals which I seem to recall were cooked at a kitchen in Holt and brought to the school for consumption in the main hall. The cost of one week's dinners was 2s.1d , or in today's money, just over 10p. I will leave the appraisal of these meals to some other pupil who has survived. One thing that I do remember is that there was one desert which was made out of cocoa, and maybe some sand and cement which attracted a large demand for seconds.

We had now reached the pinnacle of Newtown Junior, the top class. 'Pop' Boulding was in his thirties but to us he looked older due to his mop of greying hair. He was not a big man but walked with long bouncing strides. We often passed him on our bikes as he strode to and from his lodgings opposite the 'Ship Inn'. He rarely showed any emotion but behind his stern face one could detect at humorous moments a subtle glint in his eye and a pouting of his lip. If anyone could motivate me, it would be him. Lessons became more interactive and whatever the subject he commanded attention. However more sweeping changes were on the way. After a few months of the first term, Mr Meek, the headmaster, retired and his successor Mr Ralph Warburton took the reins. It wasn't that we were to see changes but we were to see new things. All of a sudden, we were to see much more emphasis on competitive sport. No longer were we blue or yellow bands, we were in Houses!! The house boards took prominent position in the main hall: Corsham, Lacock, Longleat and Wraxall. I was placed in the latter and felt good about it.

Sporting activities were rapidly introduced after lessons. 'Pop' organised variations of hand-ball in the playground and a limited amount of football. As summer approached, Ralph had a cricket pitch marked out and he ran his cricket school. In front of the wickets a rectangle was marked and Ralph would insist over and over again the importance of bowling a good length into this rectangle. I think he enjoyed it all every bit as we did as he spun the ball between his hands one of which was minus a finger. Soon we had fully fledged football and cricket teams. For football we were provided with new shirts in what would be eventually the school colours, red and maroon quarters. For cricket we turned out in white shirts with our grey flannel shorts. Home games against other junior schools were played at the Flower Show Field between Holy Trinity Church and The Innox. Even the girls turned up to cheer us on. Sadly no cheerleaders in those days! Away games brought the most excitement when we visited Lowbourne and St Michael's in Melksham. The favourite venue was however a private boarding school in Bradford on Avon called Kingwell Court. After the game they would host us to a meal of bangers and mash which was out of this world. Some things never change. If Mum had served it at home I would probably have turned my nose up at it!!

Starting in May when the T.U.D.C. open-air swimming pool opened, weekly swimming lessons became compulsory unless one had the note. Now this pool was unheated and the lowest water temperature that I can remember was 8°F (sic). No fun, although during the holidays it once reached 84°F but was so full one couldn't find space to swim. At the start of all of this, I was terrified. I could not swim!! Pride also took a battering as I was designated to the baby pool. Something had to be done to overcome my hydrophobia (fear of water – not rabies!).

Mr Toombs, the Council employee in charge of the pool, would conduct the lessons. He was a short stocky man with a mop of grey hair and bushy eyebrows and always appeared to wear the same white submariners' polo necked sweater. He was a good teacher, he taught me to swim and later in life I would need to. After shivering almost to death after lessons, we would be allowed to buy a hot lemon drink for 1d. from the pool shop which also sold a variety of confectionery. The shop was run by a Mr & Mrs Stone. He also bred goldfish, watch the fish-paste sandwiches, men!!

Morning assembly now took on a new look. We now filed into the main hall to classical music played from a gramophone. These pieces had an overtone of patriotism, and why not? Hadn't we all won the lottery of life to be born British??!! I well remember Elgar's 'Nimrod', 'Dream of Gerontius' and 'The Enigma Variations' and they remain today some of my favourite orchestral pieces. Gone were the large hymn cards as we were now issued with hymn/ prayer books. Then a selected few would read the lesson. Why could some people do it so well? Take for instance, Nancy Holroyd reading I Corinthians 13, vv 1-13. Later I realised that her father was the vicar of (I think) Manvers Street Church. Maybe some home coaching?

Meanwhile back in 4A we were being earnestly prepared for the exam of our life. Part 1 was held in November. It was some kind of an intelligence test which I think all of us passed. Then in February Part 2 consisted of an Arithmetic and English paper, followed by Part 3 in April which was more advanced Arithmetic and English (no Geography or History to pull my average up!). I came through all this and in late May was called for an interview with the headmaster of Trowbridge Boys' High School, Mr G.V.S. Bucknall.

I had not evidently presented my case very well and a few weeks later was called for a second interview. This time I must have done worse, I failed. Imagine the torture of over six months when your young life was hanging on a very fine thread.

Between all this examination ordeal, life went on. Early in 1950 there was a General Election and 'Pop' decided that 4A should have its own election. And this we did. I don't know how the candidates were chosen, volunteers or press ganged but as it happened the candidates were: Alan Wakefield supported by Robert Evans,

Valerie Hutchinson supported by Susan Maulton, and Gloria Rose supported by Keith Denning. Candidates adopted their party colours and delivered their 'political' speeches on issues ranging from the appointment of monitors to the cleanliness of the toilets. Gloria Rose had a very articulate manifesto and was duly elected with no power at all since 'Pop' was still the boss!! Mind you I suspect that Gloria had had some very good home coaching as well!! Say no more.

Probably, the highlight of the year was the school's first day trip to London. This was to also be my first organised trip. Before that I had been on a couple of Chandler's day charabanc (what a lovely word) trips to the south coast with the family but this was to be a trip out with the boys! I am pretty sure that the trip was restricted to Classes of 4B, 4 and 4A, also I am rather vague as to whether any parents came along so as to relieve stress from the teachers.

We caught the steam train for Paddington from platform 3 at Trowbridge station. This was the slow train via Devizes and had probably been chosen as we would not have to change and it may have been cheaper. The engines were now sporting a new livery, no more the Great Western Railway as the year before the panacea for all travel had been created in the name of British Railways (Western Region). Most of the boys were avid train spotters and all carried with them their 'Iain Allan' spotter's books in which all sighted engines were meticulously underlined. There were the Kings, Castles, Halls, Counties and Granges and the innumerable 'nonkeys' (no name, only number).

This activity kept us out of mischief for the majority of the journey especially as we passed through Newbury, Reading and the final assault of Paddington. Within the time constraint we would be taken to the Tower of London and later to Regent's Park Zoo.

Many of us I am sure had been to Bristol Zoo before which in my opinion was far better, but at Regent's Park they had something which had appeared in every daily newspaper and that was Brumas. Bristol had Alfred, the gorilla and Rosie, the elephant which to us were household names. However, Brumas was unique at that time being the first polar bear ever born in captivity. That is what we came to see.

Travelling through London by coach we were able to stop very briefly at a few well known landmarks like the Houses of Parliament, Buckingham Palace and St Paul's Cathedral. However for the most it was brief encounters from the bus windows. 'Look, look, Nelson's Column. Missed it!!'

The return to Trowbridge was for me, and more or less everybody else, a total blur. We were all well and truly conked out, only finding enough conserved energy to rush home and tell Mum and Dad 'everything' about London.

Our year in 4A was drawing to a close. Many would move on to TBHS or TGHS and a few unfortunates who had failed would make their way to Nelson Haden. Of course my main concern was what would happen to me? For some reason, regardless of age, if one had passed then admittance to the High Schools was permitted, but if one had failed and had not attained your eleventh birthday at the start of the next school year then there was no admittance to a secondary modern school. I fell into this category. I forget who told me my future but I was informed that I would have to stay down in the Junior School and repeat another year in 4A along with Patrick Andrews. Here the fun started.

In those times our friendships were mostly confined to the neighbourhood in which we lived, although at school we all got on pretty well together. From my area, Terry Bishop, Alan Wakefield, Robert Evans, Terence Bennett, Bryan Rolf, Martin Wilson and Roger Green all went off to TBHS. The only other failure in our gang was poor David Crook who had been in Class 4 and was a few months older than me. He was therefore deemed to be Nelson Haden material. His fortune later changed and he was later given a free transfer to TBHS. I was determined to meet up with these fellows again next year. Also not to worry, new blood was in the pipeline coming up from 3A.

And so, it was another year with 'Pop'. First day of new term, the essentials had to be attended to – Monitors. The appointment was on a volunteer/acceptance basis and for a while we were back where it all started. Hands up!! The blackboard monitor, the wastepaper bin monitor (yes we had one!), the dreaded ink monitor was still an essential vocation but a dying breed, all were filled. Patrick Andrews (Andy) and I never even volunteered as these were considered too menial for us. After all we were a bit senior!! Then there were appointments (which I suppose one could put on one's CV later in life).

Sheila Barker and Susan Savage were to be the Register monitors. They were probably subject to strict scrutiny as to their integrity as in this position, the attendance record from all classes could be amended!!

'Milk monitors,' says Pop, 'Andrews, Skinner and Withers, anything to say?' Silence.

'Head Gardeners,' says Pop, 'Andrews and Withers, anything to say?' Silence.

These appointments were of a corporate nature and by no means confined to 4A. It was the whole school and that to us spelt POWER. My confidence grew immensely during this year. My failure was put behind me. I didn't fail, I was just too young!! However out of confidence sometimes mischief is created. Living in a fool's paradise, lessons seemed to pass over in favour of the offices of state. Occasionally 'Pop' would pull me into line, but at the back of my mind and with my class work in the top half, I thought and believed TBHS was a matter of course. After all what was the point in competing with Nancy Holroyd? If we had had metal work, she would have come first!! Every class seems to have one.

Milk duty was mostly confined to the mornings. The dairy would deliver the one-third pint bottles in crates to a side access gate situated in the drive to the Infants' school and it was our job to break the overall quantity down into the individual class requirements. Cliff Skinner was big and strong, nobody argued with him and therefore very important in our roles of what you might call Milk Distribution and Logistics Managers. Each class would have their own monitors (labourers) to collect from us the full crates and return the empties. The normal requirement per class was just less than two crates. Average class numbers forty-four. There were always several bottles left over after distribution and Andy and Cliff had no difficulty in consolidating the figures and they even had my bottle since as already mentioned, I hated the stuff.

Gardening duties were more demanding. The school garden was quite large by any standards. It consisted of a strip about 30 yards wide running from the street, south of the school building all the way down to the railway embankment and up to the Infants' School building. The stretch from the street alongside the school building was laid to lawn with flowering shrubs and trees such as magnolias. The area down to the embankment abreast of the girls' playground was laid out as vegetables and here we grew shallots, maize, root vegetables, cabbages and lettuce, etc. The lower part was laid to lawn with flower borders, and in the corner, were a few fruit trees, the most prolific being the crab apple. Pupils were encouraged to buy the grown produce for nominal amounts. On quiet afternoons I consumed such vast amounts of corn on the cob that I have never touched the stuff since. Crab apples were supposed to be good for making jelly jam but large quantities fell to the ground before maturity. Most ended up as missiles for passing trains.

The garden tool shed was our absolute domain. Entry by others was by invite only. Here we cleaned and oiled all the tools and racked them accordingly. It appeared that we could stretch out time here indefinitely. It was here that Andy and I tried to play the watering-can. We also let John Austin have a go from time to time. None of us had any claim to any musical talent but it was done to give disturbance to the nearest classroom which, by coincidence was 4A. One afternoon after tidying had been completed, Andy dared me to yell through the ventilation grille into 4A during lessons. Pop dispatched some poor soul to find out whom it was who had made the noise. I don't remember who that person was but he was told in no uncertain manner to report back that, whomever it was, could no longer be seen. Next morning after assembly was the inquisition. 'Yesterday afternoon during poetry, somebody made a vulgar noise through the ventilator, I want to know whom it was,' said Pop. With as straight a face as I could, I asked, 'What kind of noise was it sir?' 'Withers, it was something like a cow in pain.' The entire class was reduced to sniggers and Pop's lip started to pout. 'Sir, it was me.' 'Come out and stand there.' Out came his black biro (he always wrote in black ink), tore a page out of an exercise book and scribbled a note. 'Susan, take this note and Withers to Mrs Hayward's class.' Her class was 2B. Without malice, Mrs Hayward was thought by us to be really ancient. There was only one thing older and that was the out of tune piano in her classroom which had candlesticks!! I stayed there for two days. She never said anything to me and I never said anything to her. An excellent relationship, but very boring punishment.

Oh yes, we had the weekly music lesson conducted in the hall by Miss Griffiths. We would stand in an arc around the piano and were supposed to be enthusiastic about singing archaic songs by, to us, unheard of composers. Try 'Good morning, Gossip Joan,' on a sultry Thursday afternoon. Andy and I had been designated as 'growlers', and were kept in the back row. It was not difficult to allow our attention to roam, snigger, sing the wrong words and be general nuisances. All this came to a halt when during one lesson Mr Cyril Sparkes, class teacher of 4, floored me with an encyclopaedia to the head. His class room was across the hall and he made use of its proximity to flaunt authority in front of young Miss Griffiths. My punishments at school were never relayed to my parents but this time I could not disguise the large bruise swelling on the side of my head. Less said the better, but Dad, although not sympathetic to me, had a verbal go at Mr Sparkes.

As a passing thought, I recall that the school library was situated within the main hall and accommodated in a large cupboard surrounded by a few collapsible tables when open. Margaret Smith was head librarian and did a good job considering she was dealing with the likes of me who were always forgetting to return books on time.

Although I had very little to do with Class 4, it is worth a mention from an outsider. The theme of that class was puppets and puppets. One could not escape them. Poke your head in the door and all you saw were papier mâché heads everywhere. There really was only one thing of interest and that was a girl called Avril Bradshaw who had recently been crowned as the Trowbridge Carnival Butterfly Queen!!

Back in 4A we were experiencing radio education by way of the BBC's Schools programmes. Someone (I don't know who) would record *Travel Talks* and *Nature Study*. These would be played to us by a relatively new invention, the tape recorder. After listening to the programme, Pop would either give us ten written questions or it was a 'hands up session'. I preferred the latter as it gave a chance to offer ridiculous answers. I had always lived close to nature and learned very little from Nature Study. However, I did enjoy *Travellers' Tales* and maybe the seeds of my future were gently being sown without me realising it.

Before long it was time for the second school trip. This year we would go to Windsor. Our mode of transport was as for last year. British Rail to Slough and change for Windsor. Parents this year were encouraged to come along, This I know because

Mum came along but fortunately spent most of the time chatting to Ian Grant's mother since they had something in common, belonging to the Mothers' Union at Upper Studley Church. On the way to Windsor the train stopped at Pan's Lane Halt and Andy was almost bundled out of the carriage as most were of the opinion that this was the best place for him!! At Windsor we did a fine tour of the castle and enjoyed a splendid trip down the Thames to Runneymede where we were told King John affixed his seal to the Magna Carta. The trip was voted a huge success and it had given us all the chance to see a castle other than the one at Farleigh Hungerford.

My final punishment came towards the end of final term. To many, this may now appear childlike but in those early days our sense of fun could appear a little warped. As I have earlier mentioned, there was always a surplus of milk. With this surplus we would have competitions like who could drink the most non-stop. I believe Andy consumed twenty bottles once!! Then there was, who could completely finish a bottle, non-stop in the fastest time.

As it happened we were having one of these sessions when Pop was out of the class room and it was Cliff Skinner's turn to attempt the fastest bottle. All were allowed to try and make the competitor laugh or interrupt the flow. No physical contact was permitted. Cliff was halfway through the bottle, and all I said was, 'Drip it up, Skin!' At that time, Pop came into the room and was sprayed by half a bottle of milk. 'Skinner, you fool, you idiot, you lout, what's the meaning of this?' Without thinking, and Skin definitely had no intention of dropping me in it, he replied, 'Withers said "Drip it up, sir".'

Susan Savage was again summoned, out came the dreaded black pen and another note scribbled. 'Withers, you will go to Park Street for one week or forever for all I care. Susan will take you to Miss Wickham and you will hold her hand all the way to Park Street. Understand?'

Well, we held hands until we had crossed Newtown and turned up Wesley Road. We entered Miss Wickham's class room and the note was duly served. I remembered Miss Wickham, of course, from infant school days. Either she had grown shorter or I had grown taller as we were now about the same height. She seemed to tremble and then uttered, 'Brian, I'm surprised at you!' Why so surprised I thought, wasn't I the same poor soul who always got dished out the triangle? 'Sit in that desk there.' Gosh they were minute, designed for pygmies,

I thought. I squeezed myself into the seat but my knees lifted the desk and over it went sending the inkwell and contents over Miss Wickham's print frock. Send for the ink monitor I thought. Nothing was said.

What was I to do in this class for one week? I tuned myself to accept that it would be treated as vocational revision and nothing would be lost. By now I had completed all the written parts of my second attempt at the 11-plus and had so far passed and was awaiting the summons to attend yet another interview. At playtime, I was treated like some kind of celebrity by these seven-year-olds. You can well imagine the questions which were asked of this wise one from Newtown Junior. 'Is Mrs Miller really fierce? Are there different playgrounds for boys and girls? Who is the best teacher?' I told them. Eventually it was time for my triumphant return to 4A after one week in the wilderness. 'Had a nice time at Park Street, Withers?' asked Pop. 'Yes, very nice, thank you sir,' I replied. The lip pouted and the glint was still in his eyes. It was extremely nice to be back.

It would be wrong to omit from the tales of 4A a mention of the flirtations, young romances and teasings within the class members. I guess this was the year it all started. Some were earlier starters than others. In order not to embarrass readers, I'll give you a few names and see if you can put some of them together. Roger Cleveland, John Austin, John Smith (JEBS), Pat Mundy, Sheila Barker, Susan Savage, Joy Smith and a lot more others. As for me that's another story!!

Our time at Newtown was now coming to an end. Most of us had been together learning many fundamentals of life. We would now leave going in four different directions, TBHS, TGHS, NHBS or NHGS. Many would never see others again. There was sadness on our last day but with great expectations at our next place of learning. We were all extremely fortunate to have had the opportunity to have been a part of Newtown's history and it is only right that we pay our tribute to the teachers of our time which gave us such an excellent foundation for our future, viz: Miss Blanchard, Mrs Howard, Miss Say, Miss Wickham, Ms Cook, Mrs Rodway, Mrs Hayward, Mrs Miller, Miss Thomas, Miss Hillman, Mr Meek, Mr Warburton, Mr Napthene, Mr Ewing, Mr Sparkes, Mr Conroy and Mr 'Pop' Boulding.

Oh yes, TBHS would suffer me for the next five years.

Digging Trinity Pond 1934

Digging Trinity Pond 1934

Trinity infants staff preparing for action WWII

Trinity school photograph - Miss Blanchard on the far right - before 1947

An early Newtown Junior football team. Standing left to right: M. Paviour, M Bunce,J. Houldey,P. Andrews, C.Skinner, B. Withers. Seated: R. Cleveland, P. Hulbert, R. Lerwill, R. Bull, J. Smith

Last 11-plus examination 1973

An early Newtown Junior netball team 1980-81. Standing left to right: Lisa Green-hill, Catherine Smith, Kerry McHale, Justine Cole. Seated: Sharon Clare, Amanda Lee, Burnet Morris

Newtown Junior School staff 1980. Top row, left to right: Celia Davis, Monica Ridgeway, Kath Foster, Ann Williams, Andy Milroy, Paul Stacey, Barbara Lucas, Elizabeth Hincks, Betty Brant.

Bottom row: Lin Harris, Dorothy Amor, Lorna Letters, Myra Green (deputy head) John Hicks (head teacher), Margo Ward, Ellen Hyde (secretary)

John Hicks leaving photo 1982

Tim Hill Newtown Head appointed 1982

Roman Banquet at Park Street

Mrs E. Joan Doel head teacher leaving 1984

Mrs Veronica Parker head teacher Trinity Infants

Newtown Junior School staff 1985. Back row: Celia Davis, Mervyn Bush, Ann Williams, Lin Harris, Lorna Letters, Barbara Lucas, Andy Milroy, Brian Amer (caretaker). Seated: Paul Stacey, Myra Green (deputy head), Richard Craft (head teacher) Bella Osbourne, Ellen Hyde (secretary)

Trinity Infants Fire 1990

Trinity Infant Staff 1992. Top row: Margaret Glazebrook (secretary), Doug Smith (caretaker), Joan Rawson. Middle row: Helen Gainey, Chris Shepherd, Rosemary Geeke, Sandra Hall, Linda Mould. Bottom row: Liz Steele, Jennifer Williams, Claire Gunstone, Ann Carter (acting head), Sue Selwyn-Smith, Jo Hooson, Sue Hornby

Newtown name change 1992

Pictured with headteacher Richard Craft after voting in the election to name the newly merged schools, left to right, Hannah Kent, Gary Richards, David Godfrey and Vicky Holloway.

Newtown Junior School and Trinity Infants School, due to open as one school in September, have chosen a new name.

A total of 492 parents, teachers and pupils voted for Newtown Primary School. The alternative, Roger Brown Primary School, polled only 128 votes.

Headteacher Mr Richard Craft said: "Sir Roger Brown was the man who

was a local Victorian benefactor.

"About 19 names were suggested, but the governors rejected all the rest and narrowed it down to those two."

The name will now have to be approved by Wiltshire education committee when it meets on February 22.

"At the moment we are calling it the new Trowbridge primary school but the sooner we can use the new name the better," Mr Craft said.

Big Pit Residential Visit 1994

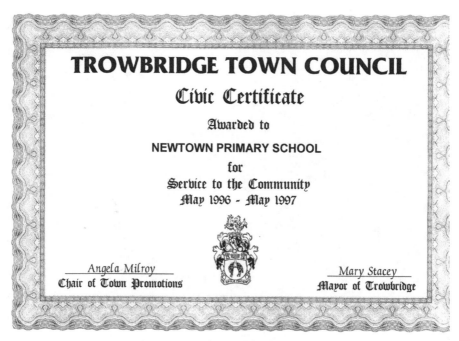

Trowbridge Town Council Civic Certificate 1996-1997

-Newtown Centenary logo

Mrs Ann Carter Centenary Celebrations

Pupils taking part in Victorian Celebrations

Mr Milroy's class at Centenary Celebrations

Centenary - former teacher Mary Stacey and MP Janet Anderson

Former pupil Elsie Keates

Carrying the Centenary Banner in Trowbridge Carnival

THE 1950s

In November 1949, Mr Ralph Warburton took over as head of Newtown. Mr Warburton swiftly set about making a number of changes within the school. These included a more formal morning assembly, the first school uniform, with maroon blazers for the boys, and maroon knitted cardigans for the girls. (Seventy years later the school uniform is still maroon.) He set up a Parent-Teachers association and the first *Newtown Junior Magazine* was published, mainly written by the pupils. There were annual school trips by train in the summer term, one to London to see the Royal Tournament was popular. Trips to the cinema to see educational films was another innovation.

Mr Warburton also introduced four House Groups for various 'competitive purposes', named Corsham, Lacock, Longleat and Wraxall. In 1953, he also had a stage built under the clock in Newtown Hall for assemblies and productions.

The junior school ran two football teams from 1950 onwards using the Flower Show Field and Nelson Haden pitches.

1954 saw a change of name in both schools, as 'Council' was replaced with 'County', the junior school becoming the Trowbridge Newtown County Junior School. At that date it had 484 pupils. Trinity became Trowbridge Trinity County Infant School.

Also in the mid-1950s the role of deputy head was introduced. Mrs Rodway was appointed deputy head of Newtown Junior, and at Trinity Mrs Sleightholme became the first deputy head.

Newtown School in the 1950s
By Jennifer Maggs (née Smith)

Newtown and Area

My parents took the job of Caretakers at Wesley Road Methodist Chapel in 1955, and we moved from Westbury into No. 38 Newtown, next to the Chapel.

Newtown was quite a distinct 'suburb' of Trowbridge at that time, separated as it was by both the railway line and the River Biss, from the centre of Trowbridge.

It was also closer to the edge of the town than it is today, with Frome Road and Bradley Road making ribbon developments towards the outskirts (without the large estates that were to spring up around the College and District Council Offices). The new Nelson Haden Schools had been built on open fields.

Newtown was a self-sufficient community. A wide range of small shops served all the day-to-day needs and with domestic refrigeration still limited, and deep freezers still part of the 'American Dream' everyone shopped daily and local.

Newtown could boast several small grocers, a newsagent/sweetshop, a greengrocer, a branch of the Co-op, a butcher, a dress shop and others. Sleightholms, the garage, was on the corner, at the top of Newtown (the site now long developed as flats) where they catered as much for the bicycle as the car. In the adjoining streets could be found wool shops, another branch of the Co-op, a baker, more butchers and grocers, etc. There was little need to venture into 'Town' unless you needed clothes or the market (Trowbridge still boasted a cattle market at that time), or something else not available in Newtown itself.

In the middle was Newtown Junior School with its solid Victorian frontage and Trinity Infants School tucked away behind like a small child hiding behind its older sibling.

My Memories of the School.

I was six when we moved to Trowbridge, and so I first went to Trinity Infants School.

I can't say that I remember much about the time I spent there except for vague pictures. I had come from a typical tiny Victorian School in Westbury (at the foot of the White Horse – now a pottery). It was small and cramped with high windows and heated by a coke stove in the corner of the classroom. In direct contrast I remember Trinity Infants School as being very large, bright and airy with a wide verandah walkway linking the classrooms. I only remember making pottery animals, but presumably we did other lessons!

I then moved on to Park Street School and Mrs Rodway, the first teacher whose name I remember. Park Street School is a square, grey school, noted (at the time I went) for its outside toilets which froze in the winter months and a small tarmac playground with great hollows for playing marbles!

Living in Newtown it was only a short walk through one of the back 'lanes' which criss-cross the area, to reach the school without needing to cross any roads, which meant that I did the journey to school and back every day on my own.

The classrooms were large and square with big wooden cupboards which held all sorts of treasures. Metal rollers that could be inked and run over your book to leave maps of all kinds of foreign countries to be coloured in. A large part of the world was coloured pink for the British Empire at that time. Other rollers held pictures of strange peoples with funny looking homes; we didn't have the benefit of 24-hour television and foreign travel to see how other people lived.

I remember learning the colours of the rainbow and then standing in a semicircle (wearing the right colour jumper!) to recite them to an audience. I still have no problem reciting the colours of the rainbow.

The rooms were divided by big wooden doors that could be slid across or opened up as required, especially for assembly. I can still see Park Street School whenever I sing 'Morning has broken', a hymn that I always associate with that school.

Along with many other Trowbridge children I have fond and happy memories of my time with Mrs Rodway.

The move back to Newtown Junior School marked the beginning of 'serious' education and the progress towards the inevitable 11-plus examination.

Education in those days was more regimented than it is today, with work being split into 'subjects'. Class work was carried out sat at desks, usually in twos, facing the teacher who wrote on the blackboard. End of year examinations were usual, and this and the style of teaching did have the advantage that the move from Junior to Secondary School saw little in the change of routine.

I remember moving from classroom to classroom for different subjects. The girls did needlework (I'm not sure what the boys did!) which consisted of cross stitch on gingham fabric, which I enjoyed, and knitting, which I hated. This was taught by a lady (whose name I do not remember) in the next room to our usual class. We also moved across the hall to do 'Dictionary work' – exercises in using a dictionary. It was enough to put you off using a dictionary for life.

I recall Mr Stacey arriving – but I don't remember being in his class. I seem to think that he taught my brother who was a year behind me.

The one teacher who made the biggest impact on me was Mr Sparks who taught Year 5. When I look back at his lessons I realise that his approach was ahead of its time and more like the style of junior teaching today. I remember more of the content of my year with him than I do for any other teacher in the junior school. We were shown home movies of his summer holiday to Switzerland (a few photos of Swanage was the best most of the class would have seen before) and a film of Fangio, the racing driver – presumably winning the World Championship. He brought in all kinds of interesting things to illustrate lessons. I particularly recall the motorbike engine and the field telephone, which when we all stood in a circle and held hands while someone cranked the handle demonstrated how electricity worked! We all brought in an ingredient towards making a Christmas pudding. My mother was then volunteered into cooking it, as we lived just across the road, ready to eat as part of our class Christmas party.

I'm sure that his enthusiasm made me realise that learning could be fun, and as you can tell, I thought he was wonderful.

From there it was on to Mr Napthene, a teacher of the old school, ready to prepare you for the 11-plus, and if you didn't pay attention he had a deadly aim with the blackboard rubber! We were conscious of being made ready for this major milestone in our school careers, but I don't remember large numbers going on to the High Schools. I know that I was upset that all my friends were going to Nelson Haden and I would have to make all new friends again.

The Headmaster at that time, Mr Warburton, I remember only vaguely as a small, but very important man who you hoped you would not be sent before. He appeared to us not to have much contact with the pupils; I suppose we were in awe of him.

General School Life.

The tone of schooling in the 1950s was set before you even went through the door. The entrances were segregated into Girls and Boys as if they were some separate beings that should not mix. What an illicit feeling to use the Boys entrance when it was Brownie night in the School hall!

Needless to say, the playgrounds were also segregated, although I don't particularly remember yearning to play with the boys; that came later with the hedge that separated the two High Schools. We played the usual mix of games – skipping, ball and counting games and the great craze of the 1950s – the Hula Hoop.

School dinners were cooked in the large kitchens of Nelson Haden School and then delivered at about 11.00 a.m. to sit and wait in the entrance hall until they were served at 12.00. You wonder what time they were cooked, and if there was any nutritional content left by the time they were served. The usual game was to try and guess what was for lunch by the shape and size of the shiny metal containers stacked in the hall.

The main hall was (and I suppose still is) the heart of the school, with the main classrooms leading off it. At that time, it had a solid wood stage with plenty of storage underneath. We had plays from visiting theatre groups and puppet shows – much like today – and I remember taking part in school productions. The school also had a choir, and we used to take part in the Devizes Music Festivals in the Corn Exchange, singing in classes with many of the other local schools.

The school also took part in the Area Sports held at Nelson Haden School; but not being an athletic child, I seem to remember spending most of my time sat on the grass at the side of the track cheering someone else on.

I do remember the outings to London. I went with my father and although I enjoyed the sights of London, being my first visit, and eating my picnic in Hyde Park, I found the Royal Tournament rather boring in places!

One of the highlights of the year was the annual craft and flower show held in the main hall. I don't know if it was organised by the school but there were a number of children's classes and we always entered. For months before we would pick wild flowers and flatten them under the carpet between sheets of blotting paper or newspaper and then, when you had found them again, mount them as a collection in a scrapbook with the proper names. I suppose such things would be frowned upon today but we did get to know the names of all the local wild flowers.

The summer term always brought a couple of changes to the school routine. One was the use of the garden as a shady retreat for lessons on hot afternoons.

It was delightful to sit in the shade of one of the trees listening to a story while being gently distracted by bees collecting nectar by your hand. A privilege of being in the top class was to have access to the garden during playtimes and at lunchtimes, and I remember many happy times making daisy chains or reading.

The other summer change was to substitute one of the games lessons with swimming lessons. This involved being marched, two by two, down to the open-air swimming pool at the bottom of the Park. Lessons were taken, no matter how cold the pool (or so it seemed) or come rain or shine. You were lined up on the edge of the pool and made to jump straight in. I remember, on one occasion, coming to the surface spluttering and coughing to come face to face with a frog sat in the overflow guttering around the water's edge of the pool. I don't know who was more surprised.

I did learn, along with many others, both to swim and dive in Trowbridge pool, and it was a sad day when it closed.

Newtown School in the mid-1950s drew pupils from quite a wide area. I had friends who lived in Dursley Road and as far away as the large new council estate at Studley Green, and as these areas grew, so did Newtown School. Eventually, as more and more houses began to go up, a new school was built at Studley Green for those moving into the area with the outward expansion of Trowbridge. Newtown Junior School again returned to serving its immediate community.

Trinity County Infants in the Early 1950s
By Cynthia Colin

I came to Trinity Infants in the spring of 1952 as reception class supply teacher for the last two weeks of term, but the class teacher did not return after the Easter holiday. I continued on supply for the whole of the summer term and was then appointed to the permanent post for the new school year, commencing September 1952.

The headmistress was Miss Edna Hall and there were seven classes.

The reception classroom had been built to accommodate a nursery class and was the second largest room in the school. There was an open fireplace, with high fire guard still intact, and low cupboards along the opposite wall to house the tiny camp beds on which the 'under-fives' took their afternoon rest.

There was a large wooden Wendy House with windows on two sides and a smart front door complete with a knocker – the knocker was a constant delight for the children!

Forty-eight rising fives were admitted on the first day of term and of course there were no welfare helpers in those days!

The school day began at 9.10 a.m. The first session of the day was called 'free activities'. These consisted of sand play; water play; painting; clay modelling; building blocks; drawing with crayons; colouring; puzzles; book corner. Resources were very limited. Even pencils and paper were precious, scarce commodities.

After the mid-morning break came reading/writing/arithmetic work with topic work arising from the free activities. Short assemblies were led by the headmistress at the end of the morning in the largest classroom. Meanwhile the screen that divided two of the classrooms was rolled back and the long room became the dining room at 12 noon. Dinners were delivered in containers. However, in those days many children went home for dinner.

PE lessons took place in the playground. On wet days exercise had to be improvised in one's classroom.

The early fifties were days of austerity. We didn't have Christmas parties, but in 1952 each class made its own Christmas cake from ingredients supplied by the staff and children's home rations. The resulting large cakes were put in roasting tins and taken home to be baked by the teachers.

I cannot ever remember ever going out on day trips or visits, but in spite of the difficulties I have very happy memories of those years.

Our Puppet Show
By Margaret Andrews

This contemporary piece was written for the *Newtown School Magazine* in 1950 by a fourth-year pupil aged ten to eleven. Unfortunately, I have been unable to trace Margaret Andrews to get her permission to reprint this account.

Mr Sparkes, our teacher, was talking to us one day when he suddenly said he had a puppet show in mind, and asked certain people in our class if they could obtain some orange boxes. Michael Hall and Lionel Dove said that they would do their best and obtained two orange boxes which they brought back to school. In a couple of days' time we had a puppet theatre made, with curtains at each side and we called it 'The Globe Theatre'.

First we made paper cut out figures and we put them on sticks. Then Roger Eacott made a wolf out of clay. Some other people in our class tried it and so instead of having paper figures we had clay models. A little while afterwards, Mr Sparkes thought out other ways of making puppets which we tried. Clay puppets were too heavy, and paste and paper beads took too long to make and were easily broken. We tried all sorts of ways and now we have decided that we have the best way, but it is a secret! Avril Bradshaw, Susan Stannard and Barbara Courtier made most of the puppets and soon we had quite a lot. Later Mr Sparkes got in touch with Mr Courtier who very kindly made a wooden framework for the bottom of the theatre and gave us some wood to make the top part. He also gave us some old caravan curtains and Mrs Dove gave an old curtain track and we soon had some splendid curtains on our new theatre. An old notice board provided green cloth to stick on the stage and blackout material was nailed all round the theatre. Then Avril Bradshaw and Susan Stannard brought some material for dressing up the puppets and they made the gloves in needlework lessons. Mr Sparkes was very fussy about the gloves and it took a long time before they were made properly. Then we had to make some back-cloths through which the puppet players could watch their puppets without being seen by the audience. This took a long time but was done at last by sewing some muslin to some special cellophane. These back-cloths had scenery painted on them by Graham Usher, Philip Reynolds and some other children in the class.

The theatre was lit by lamps which shone from the framework. Then our teacher brought a lot of motor car bulbs and a transformer, and we now have lots of lights which are worked by switches at the back of the theatre. Some of the lights are coloured and look very pretty.

At last everything was ready for our proper play which was a musical one called 'Peter and the Wolf'. Everyone in the class worked the puppets and three were selected, Susan Stannard, Barbara Courtier and Avril Bradshaw. The first two girls worked the puppets, Avril pulled the string which opened and closed the curtains and she also switched on the lights. The girls did not have to speak as all the words were on gramophone records and a loudspeaker was hidden in the bottom of the theatre, The second play was called ' The Magic Apple' and the actors in that play were Jennifer Shore, Joy Mintern and Avril Bradshaw.

Our theatre had been called 'The Windmill Theatre' but our teacher said that some people would not like that name so John Scammels suggested that we called it 'The Playbox' which we did. It was a pity that the name was changed because Susan Stannard had made a windmill out of coloured felt which was sewn on the front of the theatre and looked very pretty. The class drew lots of designs for the theatre and our teacher took the best one and Jean Forse's Uncle kindly copied it and painted a sign to fit on the front of the theatre.

We have had several little plays but the best one has been 'Aladdin' which was written by the class for a School Festival at Nelson Haden School. This play was chosen as the best out of lots of other puppet plays in Wiltshire and was performed again at a Public Concert at Nelson Haden School on June 10th.

Besides the other people I have mentioned, Margaret Phillips took part in Aladdin. All our best plays have had girls in them because the boys won't work with girls and do not work the puppets as well as the girls. But Mr Sparkes says that next time it may be the other way round and the boys may be better than the girls

THE 1960s

In the late 1940s and early 1950s, Trowbridge had begun to grow with the development of the Studley Green estate. Newtown Junior grew, with close to 200 pupils at Park Street. By the mid-1950s there was a junior class in the Bethesda school room as the school topped 500 and Trinity was forced into using the Wesley Road school room. The opening of the Studley Green School took the pressure of numbers off for a while.

In 1965, a new Junior School head was appointed, Mr John Hicks. He was to change the whole school outings to just one year at a time. That year 'auxiliary non-teaching helpers' became possible in infant schools and Beryl Haydock was apparently the first such to be employed in Wiltshire.

John Hicks introduced an annual school swimming sports for the juniors at the Town Pool in 1967, and a school pool was built in a former gardening area at the bottom of the playground.

In 1968, two mobile classrooms were brought in. The former allotments were eventually made into a playing field the following year, and by 1970 extensions to the boys' and girls' cloakrooms meant lavatories in the main school building.

By 1967 the schools were growing again – and Park Street came back into full use. The Junior had gone up to 429 by 1969. Then the Grove School opened and children transferred to the new school.

Trinity Infants was also affected, and the new head Mrs E. Joan Doel, who came in 1968, had to deal with changes in pupil and staffing levels.

The 1960s
By Susan Thomas

These reminiscences have come from Susan Thomas, who eventually did change her mind and get married and is now Mrs Sue Keefe. P.S. She still loves writing and still hates arithmetic!!

It was the springtime of 1960 and I was sitting in the classroom at Newtown Junior School in Trowbridge; watching the sunlight send dappled shadows across the blackboard. My teacher, Mr Napthene, was taking an arithmetic class, my least favourite subject, and my mind started to wander. This was my final year in this school and I had experienced many things here; both happy and sad!

I thought about the 11-plus examination I had recently taken and wondered whether I would pass it and become a pupil at the Trowbridge Girls' High School. Their uniform was a different colour to ours, which was a grey skirt, maroon cardigan and maroon and yellow striped tie, which I was constantly fiddling with.

Later on in the day, the headmaster, Mr Warburton, would be coming to test our reading abilities. He would bring his copy of *Wind in the Willows* with him and we would have to stand up, one at a time, and read some pages of it out loud.

Then after lunch we would probably have games, such as rounders, out in the playground. We would each be in our teams or 'houses', and mine was Corsham, which meant that I wore a red shoulder band. The other houses were Wraxall (green); Lacock (blue) and Longleat (yellow).

I sighed again ... I was useless at games, and every year when we had our sports day at the Flower Show Field, just down the road, I would dread it. One year I hid behind a tree so that I wouldn't have to do the running, and nobody noticed, thank goodness! My main love was writing compositions and I had enjoyed this since my year at Park Street School with Mrs Rodway. She had always been my favourite teacher because she had encouraged me to do what I liked best. In fact, I had recently won a prize in a competition that had been open to all junior schools in the country and organised by Cadbury's the chocolate people. I had to write an essay about cows and farms and stuff like that and I had won a certificate of merit and loads of boxes of Neapolitan chocolate bars.

The only thing that spoilt it was when I had to go around all the classrooms and offer some to the teachers. It wasn't that I minded sharing them, it was just that I was very shy and I didn't like knocking at those big doors and interrupting their lessons.

I fidgeted about in my seat. Our desks were really old and scratched and had a plank-like seat attached to the main part, and an inkwell at the front for us to dip our wooden pens into. My parents had told me that when they could afford it, they would buy me one of those modern fountain pens, in pretty colours.

I opened up the lid of the desk and took out my music book, waiting for Mr Napthene to turn the wireless on. This was another lesson that I loved: the *Singing Together* programme that we listened to once a week. Every so often we had to vote for our best tune and mine had been 'A Hundred Pipers, anaw, anaw' (or something like that!). I was in the school choir and we were already practising for the school parents' evening in the summer. We were going to sing another two of my favourite songs, 'The Banks and Braes of Bonnie Doon' and 'The Derby Ram'.

In the summer we didn't have to wear our uniform and I had two dresses what I wore, both of them red with a pattern on, and a new pair of Clarks sandals. I really wished I had plaits though, and not short straight hair with a stupid fringe.

I came to with a jolt again … The bell was ringing and I had been daydreaming again. Soon it would be time to go home and I must remember to get my coat from my peg in the cloakroom. We had a separate cloakroom from the boys, which was just as well, because they could be a bit on the rough side. One girl in the class actually had a boyfriend, but she had plaits!

I was never getting married, not even when I became a teenager and really old.

Newtown 1960–63
By Lesley Ladd

I attended Newtown School from about 1960 to 1963. The Head was Mr Warburton and the staff were Mrs Penny, Mrs Johnston, Mrs Miller, Mr Stacey and Mr Napthene.

We were all terrified of Mrs Miller who walked with a metal walking stick which she could wield pretty effectively.

If anyone knocked on the door during Mr Stacey's class he would recite from the Pied Piper of Hamelin, '"Come in," the Mayor cried looking bigger and in did walk the strangest figure'. Then the unsuspecting person would enter to gales of laughter.

The school day began with a walk to school, usually accompanied by my Mum in the early years. My sister and I didn't have school dinners so we walked back and forwards to school four times a day (avoiding the cracks in the pavement all the way there and all the way back for good luck). There was no traffic jam of parents collecting kids then as most children walked to school.

We went into school in separate boys' and girls' entrances and hung up our coats in separate cloak-rooms. We then had 'Assembly' which involved the whole school in singing hymns, listening to a reading and the day's notices. The exception to this were the few Catholic kids who were the only nominally non C of E people in the school. They went mysteriously into a different classroom, but we never knew what they did there.

There were very few coloured children in the school and I remember a particular friend of mine called Mercian Morgan came in one day and told us that her surname was now different. This completely bemused me as I hadn't come across divorce before and for ages I thought changing your name was some sort of Jamaican custom!

The school doctor came occasionally and after one visit I was told I had flat feet and for months about twenty of us had to go into the main hall and do foot exercises picking up our socks with our toes – until a different doctor came who told us he didn't believe in flat feet, so that was the end of that.

We had various inoculations, the worst of which was I think for TB. We were tested first to see if we were already immune and if the test injection 'came up' we were excused the main one. How I prayed that my test would be positive! There were gruesome stories that circulated about the jab – that there were six needles all in one, that your arm would hurt for weeks, that people had died from the jab – so that we were all terrified.

Mid-morning we had a small bottle of milk each. This was gorgeous in the winter when it was cold and full of ice and disgusting in the summer when it was warm and yoghurty.

We then had play time in separate playgrounds. The boys usually played football I think, as the girls seemed to spend most of their time retrieving the ball and chucking it back over the wall. We played rounders and there was a fad for 'French skipping' which was skipping with yards of elastic strung between two girls and the third made a sort of cat's cradle with the elastic as she jumped over it. I don't remember ever being allowed to stay in the classroom during break whatever the weather.

After the morning's lessons my sister and I went home to lunch, but most people stayed to school dinners. These were dished out in the Hall and on the odd occasion I stayed I remember being made to drink a couple of inches of lukewarm water out of a plastic beaker, because it was a rule.

After school we walked home, often visiting the sweet shop opposite the school. They did small orange ice-lollies, four blackjacks, sherbet dabs or flying saucers, all for a penny each in old money. We also collected bubblegum cards with pictures of Illya Kuriakin and Napoleon Solo, the Men from U.N.C.L.E., on them. The world was divided between those who fancied Illya and those who fancied Napoleon.

Occasionally outside the school would be a man collecting old clothes and he would give us a goldfish in exchange. There would be swarms of kids giving away their jumpers in return for a fish who died the next day.

During the summer we would be dragged off to Trowbridge Swimming Pool which was down where Tesco is now and was open-air. It had a large tiered waterfall at the entrance which made a wonderfully inviting sound but it was always absolutely freezing. The kids who lived around there used to spend all their free time at the pool and were often brilliant swimmers, but for the rest of us it was a case of ploughing slowly across the width.

Girls didn't wear trousers to school in those days, but during the really bad winter of 1962/63 the more independent minded of us started to wear trousers under our skirts so that we weren't really breaking the rules. We must have looked a sight.

One day Mr Warburton stuck his head around the door of Mr Stacey's class, which I was in, and asked 'Does anyone want to do gardening?' I immediately put up my hand only to be laughed at by Mr Warburton, Mr Stacey and all the class. They had all understood what I had not, that 'anyone' meant 'any boy'. In those days girls did sewing and boys did gardening. I shall never forget the sensation of humiliation and anger I felt at this injustice and a few years ago I gained an MA in Women's Studies! I always attribute my interest in equality matters to that experience.

Although I must admit to generally hating school I did love the books we were read. I still remember *The Family at One End Street* and the Jennings books with great affection.

Memories of Newtown 1964–67
By Ros Stenning

In the reconstructed childhood of the memory it is always a lazy, sunny afternoon. Light and warmth shine through the end windows and onto my attentive face (or at least a face resignedly feigning attentiveness, covering for a mind and soul desirous of the cool summer breeze and the scent of freshly mown grass). The streaks of light pick out the motes of dust which circle each other in erratic and puzzling orbits as I sit in the large, expansive hall. Indeed, the hall is the place I remember with the most clarity as it was multifunctional. Possessed of an ambition to be, not one, but all of the rooms in the school, the hall was something of a chameleon, its changes being facilitated by one of the crowning achievements of Neanderthal Man: the construction of the wheel. A fortuitous invention for Newtown School. I remember that Newtown had a strange mania for wheels. Not content with the traditional immobility of televisions, climbing frames, pianos and, bizarrely, bookshelves, Newtownians applied the physics of circumvolution to anything and everything to which wheels could be attached and gleefully rolled them from place to place. Thus, with the addition of a mobile book cabinet, the hall became the library, when the meal trolley was wheeled in, it became a canteen and, when the climbing frame was wheeled away from the wall, it was a gymnasium,

I remember, too, the absurdly heavy PE mats which were stored under the stage and which, with tremendous difficulty, were hauled out at the beginning of every lesson and then stowed away again afterwards. How we loved those mats. The grunts and groans, as beleaguered small children half-dragged these mat-shaped monsters to their lairs, live with me still. The PE mats, I think it would be fair to say, were pure evil. The stage itself was an extension of the classroom, and could be used for one to one tuition. I remember particularly reading to Mr Hicks, the headmaster and his asking me to spell various words.

Dipping into the jumbled memories which comprise the remnants of my time at Newtown, I remember taking part in a school play, being in the choir and entering various competitions. I can also recall that the hall took on a sinister, oppressive air for my 11-plus exam and I remember the tense silence before being told to turn over my paper. And then the panicked silence after I had turned over my paper. I also remember the intrepid school hamster (on a completely separate occasion) escaping under the stage. And winning a road safety quiz, perhaps my finest hour at Newtown. In those days, exams were *real* exams, road safety quizzes were *real* road safety quizzes and hamsters were *real* hamsters. They would have frowned on the wishy-washy, namby-pamby hamsters you get nowadays.

The school uniform was a fetching maroon and grey and the playgrounds and entrances were separate for boys and girls. We didn't much like each other anyway so that was fine by us. What sticks in my mind most of all, however, is the toilets. This is not because they were excellent toilets. On the contrary, they were a lesson in what toilets should not be. They were outside and dreadful in every imaginable way; they were dank, dark, foul-smelling and almost certainly haunted. Indeed, entire species of unimaginably horrifying creatures had evolved in their murky depths. Those toilets became my childish idea of Hell, and I was quite prepared to endure great discomfort rather than use them. Consequently, I spent three happy years at Newtown, but was always desperate for the loo.

London Day Trip

This contribution came from the *Newtown School Magazine* of 1960, and was written by a group of pupils.

The atmosphere at the station was one of excitement. Everything was hustle and bustle, with teachers looking for their parties and parents looking for their children and charges.

The great moment of boarding the train came and we started off. Out came bags of sweets, comics and grownups' newspapers, and all gaily chattered. Most of the boys spent the time of the journey 'copping' engine numbers, especially at Reading, as they passed the Southern Sheds.

When we drew into Paddington everyone suddenly came alive and clambering out of their carriages, went their different ways. Many made their way to Westminster by Underground, enjoying the ride on escalator and trains.

Some had the thrill of seeing the Queen setting out on her way to Ascot. They continued their way to Buckingham Palace where they watched the sentries stamping their feet 'wasting their boot leather'.

Many ate their lunch in the shade of the trees in St James Park after seeing as much of Westminster as could be seen in the time – the Abbey, Houses of Parliament, Downing Street, The Horse Guards, Scotland Yard and the like.

A river boat took groups to the Tower where a few found time to see the Crown Jewels, and the block and axe, a gibbet, a model of the rack and a thumb screw. They also saw the site where Lady Jane Grey and others were beheaded.

The Royal Tournament, seen in the afternoon, was wonderful with its massed bands, horse jumping and other spectacular things which, in spite of accidents to a sailor and dispatch riders, everyone enjoyed.

We all had a delicious tea before setting out for Paddington to make our journey homewards. We were all in the highest spirits when we arrived at Trowbridge at 9.35 p.m. at the end of a happy day.

THE 1970s AND 1980s

In 1970, Dorothy Amor became the first Welfare Assistant at Newtown Junior School, apparently, she was the first in Wiltshire.

That decade saw Trinity Infants grow to twelve classes, two in the Trinity Hall. The big end classroom, later demolished because of subsidence, was used as a hall. For other large events the Boy Scouts Hut along the back lane behind the houses on the eastern side of Newtown was used. When Grove School opened, the drop in numbers meant Trinity Hall could be used again.

Residential visits lasting five days were introduced in 1971, one to London and a smaller group to the Wye Valley. In subsequent years visits to Swanage and St Briavels in Wales followed.

The end of the 11-plus examinations in 1974 saw the Nelson Haden Schools combined into a mixed school and becoming the Clarendon Comprehensive School (named after the statesman and writer the Earl of Clarendon), and the High School becoming the John of Gaunt Comprehensive School after the Plantagenet prince who controlled the manor of Trowbridge and its castle in the 14th century on behalf of his son, Henry Bolingbroke, later Henry IV.

Once again numbers rose in both schools, until in 1976 Holbrook Primary School opened.

In 1977, Jubilee parties to celebrate the Queen's Silver Jubilee were held in the playground at Park Street and Newtown, and celebration mugs were given to the children.

The First Residential Visit
By Peter Stacey

This is another contemporary piece

The Journey to London

The small suburban train left Trowbridge at 09.25. Before long we reached Westbury. There we waited, sitting on our cases for 40 minutes. Several photos were taken of us. A huge goods train with 50 trucks went through the station while we waited. The engine, 'Vigilant', of the 'Warship' class was well out of the station when the last truck went through.

Our train was the 'Western Monarch'. It was pulling the Penzance–London express. We had a reserved carriage. An announcement told us that it was the carriage near the rear of the train. We were addressed as 'Newtown Junior School'. The journey took quite a long time. Our only stop was at Reading General station.

When we got to Paddington the roof was being reconstructed. Adam Faith, the TV and film star was being filmed, possibly for the TV programme *Budgie*. Mark Stillman claimed to have seen the piece on TV but this is open to doubt. The coach was waiting inside the station. Our cases were loaded in and we were taken 1km to the hotel.

This hotel looked just as I had expected it to. It was a high stone building in a long terrace. It actually was made of number 110 and 112. The address was Belle Maison Hotel, 110–112 Sussex Gardens, London W2, although it said 110–111 and W1 on our address card.

We were called out, a room at a time. We were given our key and told to leave it in the door at all times. We found out why later. The latch shut the door automatically and we found we were all locked out. Mr Bush opened the door by dubious means.

The hotel was a bed and breakfast establishment so we could not have lunch there. It was not a long walk to Regent's Park but it seemed it, as it was our first bit of walking on London's notoriously hard pavements. We sat down on the grass by the lake to eat lunch. Birds were everywhere. On land it was mostly pigeons and sparrows while on water it was coots and mallards. I had had too big a lunch and could not eat it all. The birds had a good feed.

The first day we went to the Planetarium and Madame Tussauds, and on the second day we went on a coach tour of London. Among the first sights we saw were Lincoln Inn Fields, The Old Curiosity Shop.

Then the coach dropped us at St Paul's Cathedral. The dome of the cathedral or at least the golden cross at the top can be seen all over London. The cross is 365 feet from the ground. This is almost exactly 100 metres. After St Paul's the coach took us to the Tower of London.

After lunch we went to nearby Trafalgar Square underground station. Our ticket machine had quite a job spitting out fifty-two 10p tickets. We went by underground to Kensington to the Museums of Natural History and Science.

Then we went to Trafalgar Square. There were pigeons everywhere. By the base of the column there was a stall selling pigeon corn. As soon as I bought the corn a pigeon dive-bombed it from my hand. The stall holder saw what had happened and gave me another tub free. This time I was more careful and hid the tub under my pullover and let the pigeons have a little bit at a time.

The next day we went to Windsor. The Queen actually left for Canada the day we arrived. Perhaps it was a good job (for the Queen). The journey from Windsor to Hampton Court was pretty lengthy. At Hampton Court, as soon as we were allowed to separate we all rushed for the Maze. I was lost for about half an hour. I found the centre and kept finding it but getting out was the difficult bit.

The next day when we went to Downing Street …

For some reason Peter Stacey's account ends there. The assumption must be that the Houses of Parliament and probably Westminster Abbey also figured on that day. The Friday would be largely the return to Newtown.

Trinity and Newtown in the Late 1960s and early 1970s
By Andrew Jones

I started Trinity in January 1966. Due to the lack of classrooms in the school, our first classroom was the room at the side of Wesley Road Chapel, this was before the hall and kitchen were built at Trinity after I had left.

My first teacher was Mrs Colin, I remember my first day I was left in the classroom by my mother and I found some wooden building blocks to play with. I don't remember much else about that first year, Mrs Sleightholme was the Headmistress with a room at the top of the stairs.

My next class was Mrs Strawbridge this was in the room where the office is now, the only recollection I have of the class is of having to stand in the corner as I had broken a ruler!The class I remember most and the one I enjoyed best was Miss Hanks' class. This was in the room at the top of the corridor, now demolished, we did weather recording here with a thermometer on the balcony overlooking Newtown pool. We read from *Janet and John* books. At playtime we used to go to the bottom of the playground and stand by the railings and watch the trains go by.

Mrs Haydock was the lady who helped children who had had accidents, those days were the days of free school milk which was, in the winter, put on the radiator to thaw out as it was often frozen, this also warmed up the milk and put me off school milk! In those days the toilets were on the left-hand side of the main door outside, which often during the winter months froze despite the efforts of the Caretaker, Percy Lidbury, who tried to thaw them out.

I started at Park Street in September 1968, having left Trinity Infants School. My first teacher was Mrs Foster, in the room in the middle of the Park Street side. I don't remember very much of the lessons, but we sat at desks in rows with a teacher's desk and blackboard at the front. One lesson I recall was handwriting, I had to stay in for my playtime practising writing.

Memories that stand out include a visit to the corner of Park Street to see the G.P.O. in a hole in the road. We played marbles in the drains at the side of the School, and during that year we had a trip to Bristol Zoo. Some other memories may have been in the first or second year as we had one second year class at Park Street, my teacher was Miss Smith, now Mrs Green. There were four classes at Park Street then, the other two were Mrs Lucas and Mrs Adams, she was in the room next to the Library room, which in my day was the new television room. Mrs Lucas was in the far end beyond Mrs Foster's room. When we needed more space the screens would be pulled back to give us a large room. When we were in Miss Smith's class, we took it in turns to ring the bell for playtime, we used to use the inner playgound in the first year, and I still remember scoring a goal in football there.

Mr Smith was our caretaker, and he died while we were at Park Street and some of us took a wreath to his house in Park Street.

Southampton was the destination for our 2nd-year trip, we also went to Bath, as we did a topic on the Romans.

We used to go to Newtown for a Weekly Assembly, and Swimming, in the 2nd year, we often had the girls coming under the curtains into the boys' changing room.

In the first year we did a play on St George and the Dragon, at Park Street. We also performed *Dick Whittington* on the stage at Newtown. I was a Sailor Boy, this was at a School Concert when each class took turns to act or sing. The old stage had gone by 1971.

For Christmas, we had a party at Park Street, we had games then went to Newtown for tea. Another year we had a Magic Show at Bethesda School Room. We had our own Harvest Service at Park Street, then when we were in the second year we took the gifts to the elderly in the area.

In July 1970 I left Park Street for Newtown, and Mrs Macdonald, in the far left-hand room off the hall.

In those days we used both front doors, the boys coming through the door still used and the girls used the other door, near where the kiln and PE cupboard are now.

That winter each class performed an item at the Christmas show. Our class did Dickens's *Christmas Carol* and I was chosen to play the part of Tiny Tim.

We made food out of papier-mâché, goose, roast potatoes and vegetables! I had to enter the play for the meal scene on my crutches which were made from upturned hockey sticks.

We performed the play for two evenings and had to wait in the infants school while the other classes were performing, it was a long evening! All went well on the first night, but on the second evening someone forgot to put my chair at the table so I had to crouch as if I was sitting down! I had two lines – 'God bless us' and 'God bless us every one'.

One year, probably this year, for our Carol Service, we went to Wesley Road Chapel. At Wesley Road Sunday School we also had our medical examinations, standing around in the cold waiting for our mothers, dressed only in our vest and pants.

Our outing that year was to Portsmouth, to see the *Victory*.

I started piano lessons for which I had to have an early dinner, normally I went home, then walked to the Music School in Gloucester Road.

That year our headmaster, Mr Hicks, had to go away for the year and Miss Smith was in charge for the year. In September 1971 I moved into the final year at Newtown. The 4th year being the last year we were given jobs to do and we were allowed chairs to sit on in assembly.

My teacher was Mr Bush in the room on the left side of the school next to the playground. One thing we had to do was a display on the wall of the corridor that ran along the back of the hall, where now the two cloakrooms are. I was in charge of an area that showed where newspaper stories happened. We then marked on the map with map pins where they occurred.

Our trip that year was to London. I remember coming home and watching *News at Ten* showing the corner of Parliament Square where we had stood a few hours earlier.

That year was also the year for cricket. We went to see a match on the Unigate ground in Bradley Road. I was appointed Baggage Boy for the school cricket team. This involved collecting the kit from the cupboard in Mr Hicks' room and taking it to every match. We played home or away. We went to Bradford and Chippenham [Frogwell], and other schools.

That summer we also went swimming at the old Trowbridge swimming pool in Brown Street. We used to go every Monday after dinner, walking up Newtown, down Dursley Road, across Orchard Road, then along Brown Street. While in the 4th year we sat our 11-plus in the hall, the majority of us failing and going to Nelson Haden.

INTO THE 1980s

In 1982, John Hicks retired as headmaster of Newtown Junior, and Mr Tim Hill became head. Tim Hill disposed of the wooden double desks with lift-up lids, and wooden cupboards in use since at least the 1960s, and replaced them with more modern grey or mushroom-coloured chipboard-topped tables, plastic chairs with metal legs, and plastic covered units.

Two years later, Mrs Veronica Parker arrived as head of Trinity. She too sought to upgrade the furnishings and equipment.

In 1984, Tim Hill resigned as head of Newtown, but before he went he restored the bell high in the roof of the Park Street Annex which had not been rung for fifty years. The following year, Richard Craft took over as headmaster of the Junior School.

The 1980s saw increasing co-operation between the two schools with a joint concert with Parochial Junior and Margaret Stancomb in the Civic Hall, and then a swop of teachers between the schools.

Fifty years after Trinity Infants, in 1986, the Juniors finally dug their own pond in the former garden, close to the swimming pool.

In 1989, co-operation developed further with another joint concert, and a joint staff meeting of the two schools.

Sue Hornby started as a pupil at Newtown in the 1950s, but her links with the school as a teacher assistant and a whole range of other roles extended over the years, mainly with the Trinity Infants but also through the amalgamation.

A Life at Trinity
By Sue Hornby

Autumn 1955. So here I was at school left to fend for myself. I can't really remember much about my time in Trinity Infants. Mrs Sleightholme was the Headmistress, whose office was upstairs and only visited when really necessary, or for the dreaded medicals!

As for the teachers' names I cannot recall, but I remember one was very kind when my big brother forgot to pick me up one afternoon, and in floods of tears was led by the hand to wait at the front door. Another lasting memory, and not just in the mind, were the 'rush mats' we had to sit on for PE – cellulite at five! I used to enjoy milk but after either trying to hack through two inches of ice or two inches of cream (when the milk crates had been left by the radiators) my taste buds changed!

Playtimes were enjoyable – the Prattens had not even been thought of and we had a clear run. We all used to wave at the train drivers who responded with an extra puff of steam. I had the added bonus of being able to wave to my grandfather who had a garden opposite the school (where the extension to County Hall now stands).

I walked home every lunchtime, no such luxury as a packed lunch, and some days it was a wonder I returned in the afternoon – snowball fights were far more interesting!

At seven, I went to Park Street, the 'big school'. Mrs Rodway was my class teacher, a disciplinarian and much respected, especially after she kept me after school just for knocking all the chairs off the tables! However, whether through notoriety or just a very good memory, Mrs Rodway usually remembered her pupils' names even decades later, and for some reason she always remembered mine!

On returning to the Newtown building, my first class teachers were Mrs Penny and Mrs Johnstone. They shared a class, Mrs Penny in the mornings, and Mrs Johnstone in the afternoons and I think it may have been for this reason that I couldn't form a 'real' attachment to those teachers. The following year it was across the hall to Mr Stacey. Now we knew we were at school! The daily reciting of times tables, the weekly spelling tests and the obligatory facing towards the blackboard. The phrase 'cheats never prosper' comes to mind here. We were doing our end of year 'exams' – maths. I sat next to the 'class genius' Andrew Garlick. There was one answer I wasn't sure about so I sneaked a look at Andrew's answer. It was different to mine so I altered my answer, only to find later that if I had stuck to my original response I would have come out with top marks! Mr Stacey could and would not tolerate any disruption to his lessons. He would walk around with a ruler in his hand which would come down perilously close to your knuckles, and on the odd occasion a blackboard rubber would fly through the air to attract the culprit's attention.

Mr Stacey did, however, have a wonderful sense of humour, and it was with some sadness when I had to leave his class to go to Mr Napthene, who although strict, lacked somewhat in humour.

Weekly arguments were quite common amongst us, we all wanted to be 'ink monitors'. It was great fun filling the ink-wells to over flowing and then using all the blotting paper to soak up the floods. It was even more fun to roll up pieces of blotting paper and to see how far they travelled, catapulted from the end of a ruler! During the summer months the outside toilets were a great place to hide, but it was amazing how incontinence cleared up very quickly during the winter months!

Mr Warburton, the headmaster, was heard but seldom seen! If seen, usually his office, you knew you were in trouble. I was sent there once, had one stroke of the cane across my palm, and I never went there again. It was not so much the fear of the cane as much as it was the fear of my mother's wrath for getting into trouble!

We made the weekly trip to the outdoor swimming pool which was located in Brown Street. Not as though we girls had a long time in the pool though, it took us nearly the whole session to put on those dreaded rubber swimming caps!

Newtown used to hold an annual flower/craft show. One year I pestered my grandfather's neighbour for a yellow rose bud with which I had great hopes of winning first prize. Unfortunately, by the time judging came around, the warmth of the school had opened the petals and it was far from perfect – I came second! However, I did win first prize for my observational painting of a pansy.

In our last year at Newtown we were allowed to go in the gardens at the bottom of the playground (where the swimming pool is now located) and supposedly rehearse for *The Pied Piper of Hamelin*. The production never reached the stage but we certainly enjoyed ourselves rehearsing for six weeks.

We also had to sit the 11-plus exam during our final year. Desks were put out in Newtown Hall and a 'hush' descended for a couple of hours around the school. I passed the exam but failed my interview for the Girls High School, so Nelson Haden Girls (now Clarendon) beckoned. I left Newtown with mixed memories, little thinking that I would return, but return I did!

Some twenty years later I was taking my daughter to Trinity and this time parents were welcome to go into the school, and you could actually go into the classrooms without fear of being told how 'awful' your child was! Mrs Doel was then Headteacher, Mrs Colin, Mrs Ballenger, Mrs Harvey, Mrs Senior, Mrs Selwyn-Smith and Mrs Geeke being the teachers I can remember. The Head's office was still upstairs, and unknown to me all those years ago, doubled as a staff room. The staff definitely needed their caffeine after negotiating those stairs two to three times a day, a fact I was to find out for myself on becoming an E.S.A., and had to make the playtimes drinks for the staff on duty. I knew I was 'in' when I could negotiate the stairs, carrying a tray of coffee mugs, without spilling a drop of it.

In 1985, when both of my children were 'installed' at Trinity, a vacancy arose for a cleaner at the school. I was successful and started in the Christmas holidays. What had I let myself in for? The old outside toilet blocks still existed, but washing facilities were inside the school, (some outside the classroom next to Trinity Hall, and some where the M.D.S.A.'s cloakroom is now located). There was no carpet in the corridor, and only a large carpet square in each of the classrooms, the remainder of the floor being wood block, which needed varnishing every year. And those dreaded stairs which this time needed to be negotiated with a vacuum cleaner.

At this time one of the classrooms was located on one side of the Trinity Hall, and after commenting one day about the amount of paint on the floor, I was asked if I would like to help in the classroom. The following week I was installed as a parent helper, and before long I was helping all the Reception/ Year 1 teachers with a variety of tasks, one of which was to help remove the contents of the old air-raid shelters which were located at the front of the Trinity buildings. Unfortunately, valuable treasures were never found, old desks, paint pots, etc. were the only discoveries.

On Mrs Doel's retirement, Mrs Veronica Parker became Head of Trinity and many changes began to take place. The corridors became more 'user friendly' with carpeting and curtains, the classrooms were carpeted and an office was created downstairs (now the First Aid Room) although the staff room remained upstairs.

Not long after becoming a parent helper I was asked if I would like to become a dinner lady. So one Monday at midday I reported to Mrs Haydock for duty. (Mrs Haydock was then the Senior Welfare Assistant/Senior Dinner Lady.) A blue nylon 'house-coat' was presented to me and I was pointed in the direction of a classroom (the hall being inadequate to cater for the large number of children). Fear and apprehension descended upon me! Why was one child climbing up the window sill? How do I persuade some to eat at the table rather than under it? Why did I agree to this? However, after a couple of weeks and a 'battle of wills' (I lost) we had an understanding and the dinner hour passed with fewer incidents.

Eventually some welfare hours became available and I started at the 'bottom' (literally) but enjoyed every minute. Hours fluctuated every school year but gradually I was privileged to become 'under-study' to Mrs Haydock, although the 'inner secrets' of the workings of the school were never revealed to me until her retirement. Art, sewing materials, Christmas costumes, etc. just used to appear from nowhere but now I was privy to their whereabouts – I had arrived.

School records mention a pond in Trinity Infants but this must have been filled in before my time, because staff, parents and children alike helped to dig out the current pond situated in Trinity playground. Weekends were spent laying the paving stones around the pond, planting the gardens and trying to put up the fence. I say 'trying' because on one corner something prevented the posts from going in. Rumour has it that there may have been an air-raid shelter under the surface and presumably we had come across the roof, hence the reason why the fence is not perfectly straight.

The Parents Association came to the fore during the late 1980s/early 1990s with the expansion of the summer/Christmas fayres and the introduction of the very popular barbecues. I served as Secretary for about three years and it was during this time that the Association achieved charitable status. Fund raising, as now, was the main objective. Various ideas were tried and tested – a sponsored 'bounce' (an inflatable castle was installed in the now demolished classroom), a Maths Day (where parents were invited to join in – at a price of course) and when amalgamation was imminent 'sponsor' a brick!

In the latter year of Trinity I became Clerk to the Governors, with the promise that meetings only occurred every half term. However, with the run up to amalgamation, meetings took place nearly every week (twice a week in some cases) and I must admit it was with some sense of relief when I relinquished the post of Clerk on the completion of amalgamation.

However, a couple of years later, bribed with an Easter Egg, I became Clerk again, but I now find myself on the other side of the fence as I now represent the non-teaching staff on the governing body.

I have a lot to thank Trinity School for – it was my 'spring board'. The good times far outweighed the bad, but bad there was! We've had fire, flood, subsidence, 'plagues' (sometimes something different every week), I am not sure about pestilence, and the many other disasters, but on the whole the school came through.

The aftermath of the fire saw staff and parents alike washing pieces of equipment (e.g. individual pieces of Lego with toothbrushes) and furniture, in order to re-open the school in the quickest time possible. To alleviate some congestion whilst the workmen were in, Newtown Junior School opened its doors and offered the use of a classroom and its playground – a sign of things to come.

The fire also badly damaged the windows of the end classroom and these were replaced with state-of-the-art UPVC frames. Unfortunately, after only a few months the foundations were found to be unsafe and the classroom had to be demolished – another shortened holiday as furniture/equipment had to be removed, and after demolition the whole school virtually needed cleaning because of the layers of dust which had descended.

The leaking of the water tank in the loft brought the staffroom ceiling down together with water cascading down the stairs and into the cloakrooms below. It also brought a shortening to the summer holiday as Anne Carter and I tried to salvage the carpets, books, equipment, etc. again in order for the school to open on time.

The summer holiday of 1993, prior to amalgamation, was the holiday to beat all records. The end wall in the Newtown playground was demolished in order to link the two schools by means of a path. The resultant rubble and hundreds of bricks obviously needed clearing. Skips were brought into Trinity playground and hot summer days were spent wheel-barrowing rubble over an unmade path and neatly stacking at least 500-plus bricks at the bottom of Newtown playground. Unfortunately, because work was behind schedule with regard to the main link building, the sole access was the unmade path. Work frantically started laying the paving bricks and obviously the 500 bricks had to be removed as they constituted a safety hazard. Once again they were moved and 'lovingly' stacked on the balcony but not for long! On closer inspection the balcony itself was subsiding and considerable under-pinning would be required. The Sunday before the school opened was spent moving the bricks yet again, this time to the rear of the mobile classrooms in Trinity playground.

Newtown Primary School opened as planned but the first mornings assembly passed in a complete blur for me. I was now Senior M.D.S.A., mainly responsible for school dinners, and in order to try and integrate all age groups, it was planned to have just one sitting. The first morning was spent trying to work out who should sit where hoping that the table numbers would coincide with the number of children. Lunchtime arrived and we coped but the sheer volume of numbers meant that dinners had to be taken in two sittings.

Christmas lunch meant catering for some 300-plus children with only an hour to get them 'fed and watered'. Obviously, we ran over time, but not by much, and another landmark had passed.

The school has now been in existence for nearly seven years; more walls have been demolished, and many improvements have taken place. It too has survived many traumas – two OFSTED inspections, boiler failures in the depths of winter, a flood in the front entrance and various burglaries. But, as in the past, the school has survived and continues to go from strength to strength, and I feel proud to think that I have played some small part in its success.

My Experiences at Trinity and Newtown School in the 1980s & 1990s By Nicola Hall

My first experience of education was at Trinity Infants School, in the autumn of 1988, and it was quite a daunting experience because despite the fact that the school only had eight classrooms, it seemed huge when you were that small. Generally, my time at Trinity was fairly uneventful, but I have a few fond memories of those three years, the assemblies where we would sit on the floor of the hall and read the words of the songs from the handwritten flipchart at the front, and how proud you felt when it was your birthday and you got to go and stand up in front of everybody and show your birthday cards. But there was one main event at Trinity that will always stick in my mind, the fire in one of the Pratten huts in 1990. The fire started in my classroom and most of the work that we had done during the year was lost. A temporary classroom was set up in the hall, and so it was divided into two, with one class at one end and one at the other, which was quite cramped but exciting!

The beginning of Year 3 brought the change from Trinity Infants to Newtown Junior school, and the first year I spent at Park Street, which was the annexe of Newtown down the road. It was small but very old, with high ceilings and outside toilets. It was set on the main road, and we used to play games where we would race the cars that drove past the playground. Every week during the summer we would walk down to Newtown to have swimming lessons in the pool, which was outside and absolutely freezing, even when the sun was shining! Park Street stopped being used as an annexe the year after I left, and to commemorate it, we had a small party and a ceremony where one of the teachers got to ring the old bell that was mounted in the roof. Unfortunately, she pulled the rope a little too hard and it snapped, which caused much hilarity amongst the pupils, and much embarrassment from the teacher responsible.

There are many events about my time at Newtown that evoke memories, such as when I began violin lessons in Year 4. I was one of the few pupils in my class to have music lessons in school and my teacher at that time was very enthusiastic about my playing. And so, every week when I came back from my lesson, she would make me stand up in front of the class and perform a very wobbly and off-key version of whatever I was playing at that time, to thirty bored ten-year-olds. It was from this that I gained my dislike of playing solo in front of people.

Newtown Junior School and Trinity Infant school amalgamated when I was in Year 5 to become Newtown Primary School and I remember how my friends and I used to shout through the railings to the builders who were making the link between the two schools.

We had to draw pictures of our views of the building work as it took place, and we had a competition between Years 3 to 6 to find the best two pictures. My picture won one of the prizes and I remember having to go up in assembly and collect my box of Maltesers chocolates! We also had a photo that was taken of all the Junior School pupils in the summer to commemorate the closing of the school, and I remember feeling so proud because I was one of the oldest ones in the photo and I got to stand near the top of the photo instead of at the bottom like I usually had to because I was so short! It didn't really feel any different being part of a bigger school, although we were allowed from then on to help with the younger pupils during our lunchtimes, which helped to fuel my ambition to become a teacher. I was a member of one of the last years to have attended Newtown Junior School, which formed a large part of my early life.

Every year, the Year 6 pupils were given the privilege of going on a residential trip somewhere, and every year group before ours had gone to Swanage, but when our turn came, we instead went to Danywenallt in Abergavenny in Wales. We arrived in less-than-perfect weather conditions (expected for the time of year, but solid wind and rain for five days are more than off-putting for a group of eleven year olds!) but we succeeded in having a thoroughly enjoyable week, except for one particularly nasty experience where we were halfway up the side of a mountain in the freezing cold and pouring rain. I hastily opted out of that one, preferring to go back and have a shower before the hot water ran out. We got to see a lot of the local wildlife, by trapping (humanely) small voles and mice, and we also walked behind a waterfall, which was a truly amazing experience (if a little damp!). We were given picnics to take out with us during the day, but the evening meals were served back at the centre. The food was generally very nice, except one night's pudding, which consisted of a rather foul tasting banana and toffee flavoured yoghurt, which only one person on our dinner table actually enjoyed! So that night, she got eight puddings while the rest of us went without!

I have lots of fond memories of my time at Newtown; too many to be written down, but my years there formed a large and enjoyable part of my life. I still have many friendships from the school that are still going strong today.

INTO THE 1990s AND THE NEW MILLENNIUM

By Andy Milroy, former teacher

As is obvious in the introductory history, the 1990s were a hectic time for both schools as the prospects of a merger became a reality. When the building work began on the linking block that would join the two schools together physically, the clay underlying the playground was revealed. We obtained from the builders a chunk of that clay.

By then, Newtown Juniors had a kiln to fire pots and other clay models. My class began to make pots from the Newtown clay and when they dried, we placed them carefully in the kiln. The kiln was then put on and the long wait to see what happened took a couple of days. When the cooled kiln was opened, we saw what had happened – the pots had all exploded and were in pieces! Obviously more refined clay was needed for pots ...

I was in charge of preparing for the Centenary celebrations and I quickly became aware that much of Trowbridge was run by a Newtown mafia of former pupils. Permission to use the Town Park was gained from a former pupil, permission to march from the Park to the School came from another former pupil.

Janet Anderson MP, Minister for Tourism, Films and Broadcasting, was invited as a former pupil, her father had run the Labour Club at the end of Newtown. On the day she reminisced with a former classmate, Trevor Porter, the *Wiltshire Times* photographer who was covering the celebrations. Another former pupil, Radio Wiltshire presenter Sue Davies, came to the large Celebration Exhibition in Newtown Hall. Her mother had been a cook and provided school diners.

Former classmates who had not seen each other for fifty years came to the Exhibition and shared stories, interested in the changes to the school and delighted in the way much of it was how they remembered.

One strand of the Newtown story that has not been brought out thus far is that because the school was non-denominational parents from a wide variety of backgrounds sent their children to the school. In the 1950s, when the Jamaican and Afro-Caribbean families first moved to the town, the children joined the school along with children from Hungary who had fled their native country following the Uprising of 1956.

The factories and mills were always looking for new workers – Bowyers, Airsprung and other businesses up on Canal Road and soon we had Macedonians too (they refused to be called Yugoslavs!), to add to the Italians and Czechs. Movement of people from Europe seeking work in Trowbridge is nothing new. Dutch weavers came to Trowbridge in the 17th century!

In the early 1970s the Moroccans arrived, brought over by Ross Chickens because they could not find any British workers willing to work in their factory. Using French as an intermediate language, the teachers taught the new children until they gained some English and soon they in turn were acting as translators for their parents.

Each new crisis, each new influx of refugees brought new faces to the school, Somalia was a classic example.

Most recently it has been the Poles. Trowbridge has had a strong and vibrant Polish community since the end of the war. After the conflict, many Poles had been housed in huts on Keevil airfield. Over time they moved out to work, bought houses and established their own community in the town – Trowbridge is the centre of a very large Polish parish, centred on the Polish Club in Waterworks Road. Consequently, other Poles have come to the town, attracted by this existing community.

Other schools had to struggle to provide multicultural education, we just involved the children.

In the book it is a repeated fact that Newtown School provided the founding population of many other primary schools within the town – Studley Green, The Grove, Hollbrook, Walwayne Court and Longmeadow. If you look at a map, and plot the location of those schools, Newtown is in the centre, like the hub of a wheel with other primary schools like spokes around the edges. This, in part, has been because the school was intended from the start to be non-denominational, to be open to all. It soon became a council school, and therefore the other council schools – later county or community junior schools – came from this founding impetus.

I left the school in 2003. I was sad to go, my retirement was not voluntary. However, moving around the town over the years since then, the affection and respect in which the school and its staff are held by those living in Trowbridge or spread across the globe, is obvious.

This book is designed to be a celebration of both the school and its pupils, of what the school means to the town and will continue to mean.

W Roger Brown portraiit
courtesy Rosemary Hawkes

Harry Sanders in uniform

NEWTOWN BRITISH SCHOOL.

. . *Names of Committee* . .

Sir W. Roger Brown, J.P., C.C.
W. N. Haden, J.P., Homefield.
C. I. Haden, Freemantle Cottage.
I. Chapman, Westbourne Gardens.
J. C. Hanley, Hill View.
J. E. Docking, Westbourne Gardens.
J. Usher, Hilperton Road.
E. Usher, Hilperton Road.
J. J. Hibberd, Frome Road.
W. Applegate, Hilperton Road.
W. J. Mann, Rodney House.
C. H. Woodfin, Trinity Villa.
W. Walker, J.P., Longfield House.

H. Sainsbury, Gas Works.
E. F. Hill, Bristol Drapery.
Rev. H. Sanders, Hon. Sec., Westbourne Gardens.
  „ A. J. Pearse, M.A., Hilperton Road.
  „ W. J. Packer, Wingfield Road.
  „ W. T. Gill, Wingfield Road.
  „ T. Brackenbury, Wingfield Road.
S. A. Hiscock, Wingfield Road.
J. Pearse, M.D.
F. Vince, Hon. Assistant Secretary.
Joseph Gore, Church Street.
T. A. Kingham, Bradford Road.

TROWBRIDGE, JUNE 28TH.

DEAR SIR OR MADAM,

WE desire to lay before you the proposals of the above-named Committee for the erection of the New Schools in Newtown, and to solicit your interest and support for the same.

The need for a British School in Newtown is proved to demonstration by the success of the present School held in the Wesleyan Wesley Road Schoolroom. The School was started in August of last year with One Hundred and Eighty Children, and every week since the opening of the School Children have been refused admission for want of room. The present meeting place of the School is only a temporary arrangement, the Education Department consenting to our use of the Wesley Road School only on condition that we erect a new commodious School. The Committee have decided to erect New School Buildings to accommodate Five Hundred Children, to be called the Newtown British Day School.

The term British expresses in a word the broad character of the education to be given. The Religious basis of the British School System is what is termed undenominational. The Bible is read and its historic and ethical features expounded. There is absolutely no teaching of a sectarian character.

The splendid Educational Work done by the old British School is in itself the greatest commendation of this new work in Newtown. This New School is really the outcome of the old British School, and a continuation of its principles of Elementary Day School Education amongst the rapidly increasing population of the Newtown District.

It is imperative that we should proceed with the New Buildings at once for the reason that we shall endanger the Grant to the present temporary School. We must go forward. We have every incentive for so doing. Sir W. Roger Brown has generously given the Site and a donation of £500, Mr. W. J. Mann £500, Mrs. Haden £300, Mr. J. Usher £200, Mr. W. N. Haden £150, Mr. C. I. Haden £150, Mr. W. Applegate £50, Mr. H. Sainsbury £25, Miss Haden £20, Mr. G. Lansdown £15, Mr. J. E. Docking £10, Rev. H. Sanders £10, Rev. A. J. Pearse £5, Dr. Pearse £5, and T. A. Kingham £5.

We appeal to every friend of British School Work, and to every supporter of Free Unfettered Education, to share with us the burden of erecting the New Schools. We shall require £5,000, and we believe that you will help us to realise this amount.

In the course of a few days Collectors will wait upon you to register your Contributions, which may be if desired spread over a period of Three Years.

Yours respectfully,

For the Committee,

HARRY SANDERS,

Honorary Secretary.

B. LANSDOWN & SONS, TROWBRIDGE.

Appeal for funds to build Newtown School

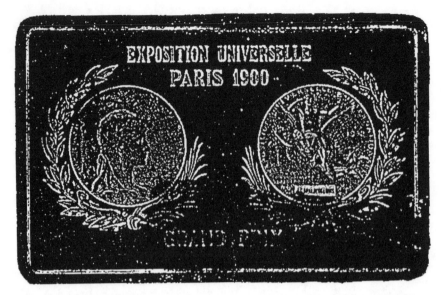

Paris Exhibition certificate

Full plan of Newtown Infants and Juniors Schools

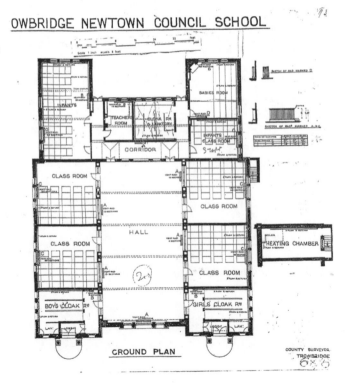

Front elevation Newtown School

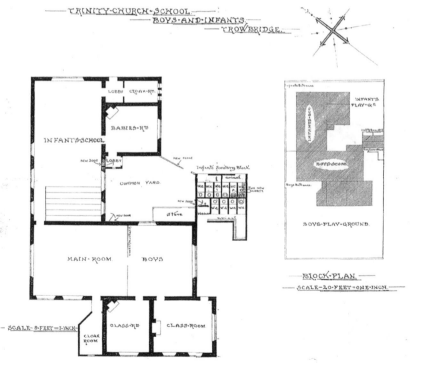

Plan of Trinity Boys School - Park Street

Newtown wood lined crawl space space

Plan of school

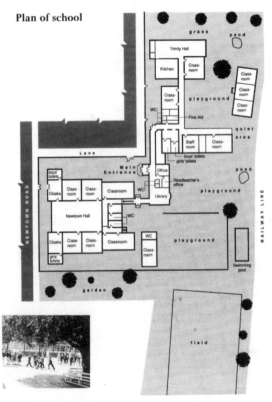

Plan of link between the two schools creating Newtown Primary School 1993

Newtown School would not have happened but for the vision and determination of a group of Trowbridge citizens.

As I have said, there were many non-conformist places of worship in Trowbridge at this time – at the Conigre and Manvers Street, and the Emmanuel, Zion, Bethesda and Tabernacle chapels and churches. There were consequently many wealthy non-conformists among the industrialists and clothiers in Trowbridge, many of whom also belonged to the Wiltshire and East Somerset Congregational Union. Key figures in the funding of the Newtown School building were also heavily involved in the Union. In 1897, William J. Mann was president, George N. Haden was a former treasurer and Sir W. Roger Brown had been the auditor for many years. This group were to be major supporters of the idea of a new non-denominational school in the town.

The driving force was probably the Rev. Harry Sanders, although the site was given by Sir W. Roger Brown and he subsequently gave £500, as did his brother-in-law William Mann. The Haden family gave £620, with £200 from John Stancomb and £250 from the Usher family.

There follow brief biographies of these major figures.

The Rev. Harry Sanders

The Rev. Harry Sanders was born at Budleigh Salterton, Devon, in 1862. He entered the Baptist ministry and was pastor of Kirton in Lindsey from 1886 to 1889. In 1895 he came to Trowbridge to become pastor of Bethesda Baptist Church, in Newtown. He became involved with the move among the non-conformists in the town to build a British school in Newtown and he was secretary of the committee that was set up to bring this into being. He was the driving force in raising the money for the building, persuading Sir Roger Brown and W.J. Mann to give their large contributions to the fund.

He was keenly interested and supportive of the school in its early, formative stages, and was a member of the Managers of the Trowbridge Council Schools (Newtown, Adcroft, Trinity Infants and Margaret Stancomb).

Harry Sanders was first elected to the Trowbridge Urban District Council in 1907. The following year he left Bethesda but still lived in the Trowbridge area. He became pastor to Zion Baptist Church in Bradford-on-Avon in 1912 to 1918, walking to Bradford every Sunday. From 1918 until his death he regularly took Sunday services in non-conformist chapels throughout Wiltshire.

Harry Sanders was also a major political figure in the town. He spoke on Liberal platforms on occasion. He was Chairman of the Trowbridge Urban Council from 1911 to 1920, a unique length of office unmatched by any other individual. In December 1917, the Urban Council presented him with a gold watch and chain and an address in appreciation of his great services to the town during the First World War. It was that year that he received the King and Queen on their visit to Trowbridge.

His special war services in connection with all sorts of organisations were recognised by his appointment as Deputy Lord Lieutenant of Wiltshire. He compiled and edited the Trowbridge Roll of Honour commemorating those who died in the First World War. This remarkable, possibly unique, publication, includes not just those who died in the war, and those who won decorations, it also described in detail the role played by the different industries in the town. Fascinatingly, the committee compiling the book, led by Harry Sanders, seem to have visited every house in the town enquiring what their role in the war had been. Not surprisingly, he was known in the town as the 'War Mayor'.

In 1915, he became a magistrate for the county and was vice-chairman of the Trowbridge bench.

He was also the driving force behind bringing an up-to-date fire engine to the town. An unparalleled three-day bazaar was held to raise the money for the new engine, which raised £700. Another bazaar was then held to fund the cost of a fire station to house the engine. The fire engine itself was named after him as the 'Harry Sanders'.

He played bowls for Wiltshire many times, and was a keen supporter of the Warminster Golf Club. He was very interested in natural history, particularly birds and flowers. He never married.

He died on 18 September 1929 at the age of sixty-seven, and his coffin lay in state in the Bethesda Baptist Church for a week and hundreds of people came to pay their respects. The headlines in the newspapers of the day were 'A Town in Mourning'. An immense number of religious and other organisations were represented at his funeral, which was one of the largest ever seen in Trowbridge. There was a wreath from the staff and scholars of Newtown School, 'In affectionate remembrance of a true and devoted friend to children'. He was very highly respected in the town. As one obituary stated, 'all his life a "people's man"' to everyone in Trowbridge'. He was buried in Trowbridge Cemetery.

Obit. Notices: *Wiltshire Times*, 21 & 28 Sept.; *Wiltshire Gazette*, 21 Sept. 1929.

Sir W. Roger Brown

W. Roger Brown was born in Bath in February 1831, but his family roots were in the Trowbridge area. (His full name was William Roger Brown, but he always preferred to use his second name.) His grandfather, Roger, a weaver, had latterly lived at the Brickplat, off Union Street in Trowbridge.

His uncle, Samuel Brown, in the late 1830s began manufacturing cloth, and in 1842 was using parts of factories in Yerbury and Silver Streets in Trowbridge. He tried to expand his cloth manufacture by buying Court Mills in 1845 for £2,800, borrowing most of this money. When the bad depression in the cloth industry came in 1847 he was driven into bankruptcy. He survived this setback, and by the following year was back in business. He brought his nephew, Roger Brown, from Bath to work in the business at the age of sixteen, probably because he had only daughters, who were regarded in those days as unsuitable to run such a business.

By 1851 the business was one of the biggest in Trowbridge, employing some 500 workers. When Samuel Brown died two years later, Roger Brown, then only twenty-three years old, had to take over the business. His uncle had been a very successful businessman, and left Roger £500 and the option to rent both machinery and factory at a fair rate.

Roger Brown brought in an experienced partner, a Welshman called Michael Palmer, and the new firm, now called Brown and Palmer, entered the business. He also visited the northern textile areas in Yorkshire and Lancashire, studied their methods and decided to increase the mechanisation of his Trowbridge mills. This was to be a key factor in ensuring the success of his firm, and the prosperity of the town during the latter half of the 19th century. Mechanisation and the use of steam power was essential in Trowbridge because the Biss was not suitable for the use of water-powered machines. This meant that Trowbridge had a head start over its rivals in the woollen trade.

Times were now improving and there was an increasing demand in the trade for traditional materials such as broadcloths and cassimeres, as well as a wide range of coloured and fancy woollen cloths.

It was at this time, in 1857, that Roger Brown made the shrewd move of marrying his eldest cousin, Sarah, and two years later the couple were prosperous enough to build the fine house of Highfield, perhaps Trowbridge's finest Victorian mansion. (Now Fieldways Health Club.) The Browns never had any children.

The new firm began to invest in plant and the most up-to-date machinery, with a new power-loom shed at Court Mills, and then adding Ashton Mill, a new factory close by in 1860. It was then that they also bought Courts Mill from the trustees of Samuel Brown for £8,000. The business was very successful, and at one point there were 1,000 operatives working at Ashton Mill.

Roger Brown also made money from speculation. He was careful with his money and built up a substantial fortune and made a considerable investment in land, buying large properties at Seend, the Cutteridge estate, the manor of Beckington and Seymour's Court Farm, all this for some £62,000. As a result of this he became an active cattle breeder and farmer in later life. He put forward and supported the establishment of the Trowbridge Cattle Market, partly because of this.

He was active in public life, being a Chairman of Trowbridge Urban Council (1896-98) and one of the original county councillors. When he first stood he had the largest poll and the biggest majority in the county. He was High Sheriff of Wiltshire in 1898–99, and also Deputy Lord Lieutenant of Wiltshire. He stood unsuccessfully for Parliament three times, but it was the generosity with which he supported the local community which is best remembered.

To commemorate Queen Victoria's Jubilee, he gave the Town Hall to Trowbridge, and also the pleasure gardens at the rear of the building. (This building was also used for the meetings of the county council when it was first formed. This fact, together with the easier access by train, eventually resulted in Trowbridge becoming the County Town of Wiltshire.)

According to the booklet *Personal Recollections of Old Trowbridge* by an old Trowbridgean, published in 1979, Roger Brown's weavers 'used to say that they gave Trowbridge the Town Hall, as it was the custom to pay some sum, 2/6 or 2/9 from their wage, which was a fairly large amount in those days ... Sir Roger Brown was the only one of the [mill] owners who deducted this sum and employees considered the accumulation totted up in time to the cost of the hall.'

Shortly before 1901, Roger Brown had constructed and endowed two blocks of almshouses, each stone roofed with tiles, for three inmates, in Polebarn Road. These were called the Lady Brown's Cottage Homes, after his late wife.

He was one of the founders and supporters of the Trowbridge Cottage Hospital. When it moved to the site in the Halve (where the clinic now stands), he gave two houses to extend the site. He was secretary to the Cottage Hospital for many years. One of his last acts was to present the hospital with some cottage property as an endowment, and in his will he bequeathed to the hospital £1,000.

Also in his will he bequeathed to the parish council £250 to invest and apply for the purchase of coal for the deserving poor at Christmas time. This legacy was invested and the annual dividend amounted to £6:11s. In 1902 there were 31 beneficiaries, each receiving two hundredweights of coal. A further £250 went to the 'Queen Victoria Jubilee Widows' Fund' for poor, aged widows.

Earlier in the late 1890s he also gave the site of the Newtown British School, of course, and £500 towards its construction. In his speech when he laid the foundation stone of Newtown British School in 1900, Sir Roger Brown made clear the aims in building the new school: 'that the children of this country should be placed in such a position that they should not be handicapped by those with whom they competed. As to citizenship ... If there was anything better more than another that made a good citizen it was to know how he was to use his political power; and [Sir Roger] did not see how one could do so unless he was properly taught in his youth.'

He was knighted in 1893 by the Liberal government, probably for his good works and his political services.

Harry Sanders made the following comments about Sir Roger Brown's philanthropic nature in 1902: 'He was not an indiscriminate giver to every caller. His charity was thoughtful. He would take great pains to make sure that the case seeking his aid was deserving ... Sir Roger simply detested the professional beggar.'

He died in May 1902, and the tributes printed in the local papers give an impression of the impact he had made on the town, and the respect in which he was held: 'Living from his earliest childhood days in Trowbridge, being intimately associated with its people, sympathising with them both in their joy and sorrows, knowing their everyday needs, and always ready and anxious to hold out a helping hand where their welfare was concerned.' 'He was just if narrow; generous if parsimonious in small matters. Shrewd, honourable, kind-hearted, saving, hospitable.' Another obituary commented upon his close connections with Trowbridge: 'Having acquired his wealth in the town, he was too loyal to desert it, but endeavoured to make it a county town, happy and prosperous.'

Obituaries appeared in the *Devizes Gazette*, 15 May 1902, and the *Wiltshire Chronicle*, 17 May 1902.

William J. Mann

William John Mann was born on 14 July 1848, son of the Rev. Thomas Mann, the Minister of the Tabernacle Church from 1839 to 1894. In 1870, he paid £2,400 and a further £400 to join the firm of solicitors established by Rowland Rodway, another son of a non-conformist minister, thus bringing into being the firm of solicitors of Rodway and Mann. In 1877, Rowland Rodway's nephew, Edward Burchell Rodway joined the firm, which then became known as Rodway, Mann and Rodway, despite the fact that Rowland Rodway retired in 1878. The firm eventually became Mann & Rodway, then subsequently Collins, Mann and Rodway in the 1880s. In 1909, the firm became Mann, Rodway and Green, when William Herbert Green, a former clerk at the firm, became a partner. This firm existed as a separate firm of solicitors until very recently.

William Mann had no real need to work as a solicitor, especially after his marriage, but presumably did so as a 'hobby' and was therefore known in the profession as a 'gentleman solicitor'. He was very active on various committees (for forty-four years he was clerk to the Trowbridge Magistrates) and as a County Council Alderman, and consequently only handled the important clients, leaving the more mundane work to his partners.

His wealth came from his close connections with the Trowbridge woollen industry. On 8 June 1876 he had married Julia Brown, one of the heirs of Samuel Brown, a wealthy clothier. (The fact that William Nelson Haden was a groomsman at the wedding shows the closeness of the wealthy non-conformist families in Trowbridge at this time.) Another of Samuel Brown's daughters, Sarah, was married to W. Roger Brown, who had taken over his uncle's clothmaking business. Roger Brown had no children and William Mann became his heir, and inherited Highfield House on the former's death in 1902.

All his life William Mann was closely connected with the Tabernacle Congregational Church at Trowbridge, where his father was minister for over fifty years. He was the Honorary Legal Adviser to the Wiltshire and East Somerset Congregational Union and in 1897 the president of the Union. The following year, Thomas Ball Silcock, the architect who was employed to design Newtown British School, succeeded him as president of the Union. Both the Mann and Haden families were represented at Silcock's funeral in 1924.

Both William Mann and Roger Brown were great supporters of the proposed new British School in Newtown. They both donated £500 to the building fund. The former chaired the opening ceremony for the school in 1901. Education was one of his interests for many years. He was Chairman of Managers of the British Boys School at Adcroft from 1904, and of the Trowbridge Council Schools (Newtown, Adcroft, Trinity Infants and Margaret Stancomb) managers from 1909 to 1934. His interest in education also led him to becoming Chairman of the Wiltshire Education Committee during the First World War.

He was secretary to the Trowbridge Cottage Hospital, 'for which he did much exceedingly good work'.

William Mann had one son, Col. W. Horace Mann, and three married daughters, who survived him.

In politics he was a Liberal, and was a Wiltshire County Councillor for over twenty years. In his late years he became a supporter of the National Government.

The *Wiltshire Times* obituary stated: 'Mr Mann had for over half a century filled a place in the public, official and religious life of Trowbridge, which was unique and which it is not probable will ever again be filled by one man. Upright in character as he was in carriage, a man of supreme integrity and the essence of courtesy in all his dealings with men and women of all sorts and conditions.' He was known as 'Willie Mann' to the older residents of Trowbridge, and well respected by those who knew him. He died on 12 December 1936, at the age of eighty-eight, and was buried at Trowbridge Cemetery.

An obituary notice also appeared in the *Wiltshire Gazette*, 17 December 1936.

Charles Ingram Haden

Charles Ingram Haden was born on 2 June 1863. He was the youngest grandson of George Haden, an experienced steam engine erector who had worked for the Birmingham firm of Matthew Boulton and James Watt. In 1814, George Haden came to Trowbridge to install an engine in a local mill and was persuaded by local clothiers to stay in the town to maintain their steam engines. Together with his brother James, George Haden was soon making steam and warm air heating systems, for which the firm became famous worldwide. Among the buildings in which their systems were installed was Windsor Castle.

Charles Haden became a partner along with his older brother, William Nelson Haden, in the family business which by then was run by their father, George Nelson Haden. His role was to travel the world to give personal supervision to many of the large contracts for heating and ventilation engineering in large government buildings, public institutions, etc., often spending many months in those countries.

Charles Haden still found time to become involved in public life. He was treasurer to the committee which raised the funds for the Newtown British Schools at the end of the 19th century, and was a member of the managers of the local Council Schools, Newtown, Trinity Infants, Adcroft and Margaret Stancomb for many years. On the retirement of William Mann as chairman of this body in 1934, he was chairman until his death in 1947.

Amongst his other roles, he was treasurer of the Tabernacle Church for thirty-six years. In 1938, he paid for the reconstruction of the Tabernacle cottage almshouses near the entrance to the church, in memory of his wife,

Rosa M. Ingram Haden. He was also a prime mover in the transfer of the Cottage Hospital from the Halve to its present Adcroft House site.

He was a member of the County Education Committee, and for many years chairman of the local magistrates. Charles was an active member of the Institution of Heating and Ventilating Engineers, being made president in February 1910. He gave as his presidential address, 'Ventilation of Schools'.

Charles Ingram Haden was married three times. He died at home on 24 May 1947. 'Trowbridge is poorer for the loss of the last Haden of his generation and one who made the welfare of the town his concern,' stated his obituary in the *Wiltshire Archaeological Magazine*. His obituary also appeared in the *Wiltshire Times*, 31 May 1947.

The architect for the new school was to emerge from the same group and was obviously known and trusted by them, being another non-conformist.

Thomas Ball Silcock and Samuel Sebastian Reay

The architects of the Newtown British School were Thomas Ball Silcock and Samuel Sebastian Reay.

Thomas Ball Silcock was born on 19 September 1854 at St Margaret's Place, Bradford-on-Avon. He went to school at the British Schools in Bradford, and then on to Bristol Grammar School. In 1869, he left school and became a clerk in the North Wilts Bank at Marlborough. Bored with the mundane routines of bank work, when he moved to the Swindon branch he studied for a BSc degree. In the process of this, he and a friend of his, another student, blew up a kitchen range when doing practical chemistry!

He was first articled to Mr Spackman of Bath, and then in 1877 started business on his own account as an architect and surveyor. He was married in 1881 to the daughter of the minister of the Argyle Congregational Church in Bath, where he was superintendent of the Sunday School.

He first appears in the Bath Directory of 1888–89 as a land agent and surveyor with offices at Octagon Chambers, 46 Milsom Street. He later lived on Widcombe Hill.

He became in later life chairman and subsequently president of the Wiltshire and East Somerset Congregational Union. It is almost certainly through this body that he met William J. Mann, who was at one stage its legal adviser. Mann, of course, was one of the major contributors to the Newtown British School building fund, and would have thought of Silcock when the committee was seeking an architect for this non-denominational school.

Silcock's two greatest interests were housing and education. As a member of Bath City Council, he apparently 'converted an unsympathetic City Council to the imperative duty that lay before them to improve the housing of the poor'. At a public meeting he stated his view that 'Education is the one thing of importance to everyone. It makes all the difference to one in life.'

Politically he was a Liberal, and was an Alderman on Bath City Council for some eighteen years. During the period when Silcock was working on the Newtown British School he was also mayor of Bath City Council. He subsequently became mayor for a second term in 1910–11. From 1906 to 1910 he represented the Wells constituency in Somerset in Parliament, as an MP. (He was the first Liberal MP for sixty years to represent Wells.)

Among other buildings he designed locally were Fitzmaurice School, Bradford-on-Avon in 1897, and Hillside House, Frome Road, also in Bradford-on-Avon.

His partner, Samuel Reay, was born in Newark-on-Trent, Nottinghamshire. He began his career as an architect in 1884, where he was articled and eventually assistant to Messrs Martin and Hardy, then from 1890–91 to Charles Ponting, and then from 1891 to Thomas Silcock. He travelled in France during this period to study French Gothic architecture.

The partnership with Silcock began in 1896 and their offices were at the Octagon Chambers, Milsom Street, Bath. Reay passed his qualifying ARIBA examination in 1897. He gained his FRIBA in 1902.

The partners were responsible for designing the Congregational (United Reformed) Church in Sanford Street, Swindon in 1894, Pew Hill House, Chippenham (now part of Westinghouse), in 1895, the Old Technical College, Victoria Road, Swindon in 1897, Newtown British School, Trowbridge in 1900, Ivy Lane School, Chippenham in 1902, Winsley Manor House, a biscuit factory in Bath, Winsley (now Dorothy House) in 1902, the Baptist Church at Twerton, Bath in 1902, the Winsley Chest Hospital in 1903–04, the St Mary's and St Peter's Junior School (formerly the Grammar School) in Marlborough in 1905, the Moravian Church, Coronation Avenue in Bath in 1906 and the Churchill Cottage Homes in Somerset in 1906/7. In 1909, the firm designed the County Hall building in Truro, Cornwall.

In 1913, Samuel Sebastian Reay left Bath for London to became Assistant Director of Barrack Construction for the War Office, living in London at 80 Pall Mall, until his department was taken over by the Royal Engineers. He then later in 1923 practised in Bristol, where he lived at 26 Orchard Street.

Among his work in Bristol was the Fishponds housing scheme in 1919, alterations to the Academy of Fine Art, and the Cannon Marsh Tobacco Warehouse in September 1922. He is also credited with the design for the Llandudno Town Hall. He was one of the originators of the old Bath Preservation Society when Bath Street was threatened during a city 'improvement' scheme before the First World War.

Thomas Silcock subsequently moved to 26 Green Park, and in the years 1920–21 he was joined by his son, Arnold (FRIBA) and from 1922–24 the firm is listed as being at the Green Park address. By this time a long and painful illness caused him to largely retire from public work. In 1922, he set off on a voyage around the world with his wife and daughter, and returned in what seemed to be better health. However, on 1 April 1924 he suffered a heart attack and died. He was buried at Claverton churchyard near Bath four days later, following a service at the Argyle Congregational Church. Amongst the mourners were representatives from the Mann and Haden families of Trowbridge.

Samuel Sebastian Reay died at Monkton Combe in early 1933.

Sources:

Architects and Building Craftsmen with Work in Wiltshire - Wiltshire Buildings Record

Directory of British Architects 1834–1900

The Builder Feb. 1933

Thomas Ball Silcock of Bath: A Memoir by Nathaniel Micklem (George Allen and Unwin Ltd., London)

The Builder – Jacob Long and Sons of Bath

The Newtown British Schools were built by Jacob Long and Sons of Bath in 1900–01.

Jacob Long was born in around 1835. He first appeared in the Bath Directory as a stone mason and builder, living at 14 Newark Street, Bath in 1872. This house was previously shown in the 1871 directory as the address of George Long, also a builder, so it likely that Jacob Long was taking over a family business. The firm prospered and by the 1900s the firm was described as Jacob Long and sons, builders and contractors, with offices and probably the builders' yard in Railway Road, Bath.

Jacob Long last appears in the Bath directory in 1902, living at Cheriton House, Oldfield Park, when apparently he retired from the management of the firm. In the 1903 directory, George J. Long is listed in connection with the firm, who presumably was Jacob's son who had taken over the running of the business.

Jacob Long died some four years later on 13 July 1906, at the age of seventy-one.

Amongst other major building works in Wiltshire, Jacob Long and Sons also built the superstructure of the County Hall building in 1938–40.

The firm was in existence until about 1990, when eventually it ceased operation without any successor business taking over.

Colin Johnson, Bath City Archivist, was of great assistance in researching this information on Jacob Long and Company.

THE NEWTOWN BUILDINGS

Described by Nikolaus Pevsner in 1963 in his *The Buildings of England – Wiltshire* as being 'Extremely pretty … and symmetrical, in a domestic neo-Baroque,' one of his most fulsome comments in his description of notable Trowbridge buildings, which include the fine clothiers' houses, particularly Lloyds Bank. An early comment was that Newtown was 'the most beautiful and up-to-date school in the West of England.'

Thus the school was seen as a fine building from the start. At the opening ceremony of the School, Mr Bourne, Secretary of the British and Foreign School Society, told the audience that the plans of the Newtown British Schools building had been exhibited first at the Education Exhibition in London and then subsequently at the Paris Exhibition of 1900. There the collection of material had been awarded a diploma and the Grand Prix. Mr Bourne said he would have liked to have shown them the gold medal which represented that prize, but they were told by the commissionaires that if they wanted the medal they would have to pay for it, and it cost 720 francs to purchase it!

The Exposition Universelle of 1900 was the world's fair held in Paris, France, and was visited by nearly 50 million people. Countries from around the world had been invited to showcase their achievements. The Grand Prix diploma shown is a copy of one actually awarded at the Paris Exhibition, and it is very likely that the Newtown plans were awarded one very similar to that.

The school still appears in the Department of the Environment's list of Buildings of Special Architectural or Historic Interest.

When the school was opened in 1900 it was said to be of the 'central hall' type, that meant it was designed so that the head teacher could watch each classroom, without the children in one room being able to see those in another. It was warmed with hot-water pipes. 'The school was considered both in the design of its buildings and the methods of its teaching to be in the forefront of educational progress,' *Wiltshire Times*, 30 March 1901.

The Ventilation System in use in the Newtown Building

The ventilation system in the Newtown building has raised considerable interest from builders over the years. In the cupola or pepperpot belfry there was originally a gas ring. When this was lit, it drew the air up through the vents in the walls, along wooden lined channels or shafts, to the crawl space and the gas ring. The idea was to remove the stale air from the Newtown building, drawing in fresh air from outside.

In summer two large trapdoors were opened in the crawl space above the ceiling by using the ropes that hung down from the ceiling in front of the large windows at either end of the hall. When these were closed in the autumn to conserve heat, the bangs reverberated through the whole school. These ropes and the holes into the ceiling could still be seen in 2000.

This system is apparently unusual. It is uncertain whether the idea came from the architects, Silcock and Reay, or from the central heating/ventilation contractors, G.N. Haden and Sons. The latter were a local firm of course, and Charles Ingram Haden, one of the family, was the treasurer of the fundraising committee for the Newtown School building. Hadens were, of course, central heating engineers of national renown, having pioneered the development of the system, installing systems in Windsor Castle and St Paul's Cathedral. Intriguingly, Charles Ingram Haden's presidential address to the Institution of Heating and Ventilating Engineers in 1910 was on the 'Ventilation of Schools'. Apparently it was Hadens who installed the central heating system.

The gas ring and crawl space could be accessed by the small circular window/hatch high in the wall in the central Newtown building. This involved placing a ladder on the flat roof of the section of the building at the back of Newtown.

The photograph shown was taken around 1983–84, when Tim Hill was the headmaster, and Brian Amer was caretaker. Note the way that the crawl space and ventilation shafts/channels are all lined with wood.

A bell would have been rung by a pupil or member of staff pulling the bell rope to alert pupils in the nearby houses that it was time for school. This was in an era when clocks and watches were a luxury reserved mainly for the wealthy and middle classes. The hole for the bell rope in the ceiling can still be seen in the hall.

The Infant School Building

A new building on adjacent land to the Newtown School to provide places for 200 infants in five classrooms was decided upon in 1926, and expenditure of £4,450 authorised next year.

The new infant building consisted of two wings at right angles; the one parallel with Newtown School had two classrooms, the other three. The building framed the playground and alongside the playground side the verandah ran. Across the playground were the outdoor toilets for the children. The cloakrooms and washbasins were in the angle between the two wings. On the first floor was the staff accommodation.

Access to the classrooms was via the open verandah. Such open-air schools were first conceived earlier in the century as a way of tackling tuberculosis, later the focus shifted to more general health issues. The idea behind them was very simple – children would get as much fresh air as possible, spending much of their day outside.

However, the open verandah proved problematic. The draughts coming through the open passageway into the school were such that parents complained that they caused the children's coughs and colds. A year after the school opened, a suitable door to lessen the draughts was proposed. However, the problems still continued. Even ten years after the opening of the school, the low attendance at the Trinity Infant School was still blamed on the open verandah.

FORMER PUPILS

As Norman Rogers commented about the Newtown School in the 1930s, 'Academic standards were high, with a very good pass rate for the High Schools.' Many pupils went on to achieve success in later life. Here are a few, achieving across a range of endeavour.

Sir William Cook KCB Kt FRS – Civil Servant and Scientist

William Cook was born on 10 April 1905. His father was a guard on the Great Western Railway, and the family lived at 10 South View Terrace in Drynham Road, Trowbridge.

William went first to Trinity National Boys School in Park Street, presumably earlier going to Holy Trinity Infants, before getting a free place at Trowbridge High School for Boys. Following his education at the high school he went on to do a degree at the University of Bristol.

In 1928 he entered the Civil Service and joined the Research Department at Woolwich. He went into the study of ballistics, and with the growing awareness of the need for a re-armament programme in the 1930s his responsibilities increased.

After the war, a research and development establishment to study the use of rockets was created and he became its director.

In 1947 he was appointed Director of Physical Research at the Admiralty, and in 1950 became Chief of the Royal Naval Scientific Service.

By 1954, the British nuclear weapons programme was growing quickly and William Cook went to Aldermaston as deputy director. A successful series of atomic tests followed in 1958, 'due in great measure to the energy, executive skill and capacity for sheer hard work' of William Cook.

In 1958, he left Aldermaston to become a member of the UK Atomic Energy Authority, responsible for the growing civil applications of nuclear energy. On his recommendation the authority embarked on the development of the steam generating heavy water system.

In 1964, he became Deputy Chief Scientific Adviser to the Ministry of Defence, before eventually retiring in 1970. As Chief Adviser (Projects) to the

Defence Secretary from 1967 to 1970, he had overall responsibility for new weapon systems. He was responsible for introductory discussions with the German Federal Government and Luftwaffe which were to lead to the Anglo/German/Italian multi-role combat aircraft (later called the Tornado) project. 'It is a measure of his authority in Whitehall that he was accompanied at this meeting only by the embassy's defence attache and councellor for defence supply.' 'It was Bill Cook, respected and trusted by the German side, who was responsible for breaking the ground.'

Following his retirement in 1970, he continued as a consultant with the Defence Ministry on nuclear safety.

In 1971 he began a close association with Rolls Royce, and joined the board in that year. Subsequently he joined the boards of Rolls-Royce Turbomeca Limited and Rolls-Royce Turbo-Union Limited which were collaborative ventures with European partners.

He was also Chairman of Marconi International Marine Co. from 1971 to 1975.

He married Grace Purnell in 1929, soon after joining the Civil Service, and had one daughter. In 1939 he remarried, this time to Gladys Allen. By his second wife he has two children, one son and one daughter.

He was knighted in 1958, and was elected a Fellow of the Royal Society in 1962. In 1970 he was created a KCB.

He died on 16 September 1987. His obituary in *The Times* on 19 September commented that Sir William Cook was a man of small stature but of huge energy. He was dedicated to his scientific work.

A service of thanks giving for the life of William Cook was held at St Clement Danes Church in the Strand in London on 11 December. An address was given by Lord Zuckerman, and the ambassador of the Federal German Republic was represented, along with the chiefs of the armed services.

Maureen Duffy – Writer

Maureen Duffy was born on 21 October 1933 in Worthing, Sussex. She lived in London as a child and was apparently evacuated to Trowbridge in the Second World War. In September 1943, she was enrolled at Newtown Junior School into the oldest age group. She lived at 59 Mortimer Street at this time. She spent one year at the school, where she took her 11-plus. From there she gained a free place at Trowbridge High School for Girls, and started at that school in September 1944.The family subsequently moved to 15 Westcroft Street.

In 1948 her mother died of tuberculosis, and she moved back to London and attended the Sarah Bonham High School in Watford.

Maureen Duffy subsequently went to university at King's College London where she got a BA hon in 1956. She then became a teacher, teaching in South London for five years. During that time she wrote three full-length stage plays, and in 1960 a television play. On the strength of this, she decided to become a full-time writer.

It was suggested to her that she try writing novels instead of plays. She found this difficult, but decided to start by writing an autobiographical novel. The title *That's how it was* had been used by her for a short story she had written as a student, for the King's College, London magazine, *Lucifer*. She aimed that her novel should be based on precise observation, using concrete and evocative language.

Much of this novel is set in Wortbridge, a thinly disguised Trowbridge, as seen by an outsider, a common character in Maureen Duffy's novels.

She has published more than ten novels, five plays (all produced), a television play, six books of poetry and three non-fiction works. In addition, she has edited, translated and written reviews of non-fiction and music for *The New Statesman*.

Maureen Duffy has always been well known for the excellence of her writing, in particular for her ability to imagine crucial specific moments in her characters' lives.

She was co-founder of the Writers' Action Group, Vice President of the European Writers' Congress, and a fellow of the Royal Society of Literature. She also wrote the *Gor Saga*, which was subsequently televised.

Her published work includes:

Josie, 1961; *The Lay Off*, 1962; *That's How it Was*, 1962; *The Single Eye*, 1964; *The Silk Room*, 1967; *The Paradox Players*, 1967; *Futz*, 1969; *Wounds*, 1969; *Capital: a fiction*, 1975; *The Passionate Shepherdess: Aphra Behn 1640–1689*, 1977; *Housepy*, 1978; *Inherit the Earth: A Social History*, 1980; *Men & Beasts:*

an animal right, 1984; *Collected Poems*, 1985; *Gor Saga*, 1981; *That's how it was*, 1983 (paperback); *Londoners: an elegy*, 1983; *Change*, 1987; *First Born*, 1988; *A thousand capricious chances*, 1989; *The Microcosm*, 1989; *Five Plays*, 1990; *Illuminations*, 1992; *Occam's Razor*, 1993; *Henry Purcell*, 1993; *Restitution*, 1998.

Maureen Duffy's eighth collection of poetry, *Pictures from an Exhibition*, was published by Enitharmon in 2016.

The *Times Literary Supplement* wrote: 'Maureen Duffy has inspired many other writers and proved that the English novel ... can be fantastical, experimental and political. Perhaps it is her poetry, though, that most fully captures her range as she presses on like a medieval troubadour across barriers of genre, gender, space and time.'

Judy Farr – Athlete

Mrs Judy U. Farr, née Woodsford, was born on 24 January 1942. She went to Newtown County Junior School in 1953, being taught in Mr J. Napthene's class, in the large classroom at the back of the school, which was opposite the room of the then head Mr Warburton.

Her athletic career started at Nelson Haden Girls School at the age of thirteen, running in the sprint and hurdle events.

She came into race walking through her brother John, who was competing as a junior at the time. Her first walking race came at the age of fifteen when she competed against adults in the Southern Counties at Chiswick. She finished 5th.

She really came to national prominence when she won the Southern Inter-Counties at the age of seventeen.

Her first win in a national championship came in July 1960, at the age of eighteen at the White City, when she won the 1½ mile track walk, winning in 12:31, which was a new championship record.

She competed internationally from 1964 until 1981. This included two Lugano Trophy meetings in 1975 and 1979. The Lugano Trophy meetings were the world championships of race walking of the time. Her later international experience included World Veterans Championships in New Zealand and Australia.

Judy was also one of the pioneers of women's marathon running in Britain. She was to run the marathon as an England international, in a Home

International race at Milton Keynes, during the same period that she was competing for Great Britain in race walking.

She had actually started running in 1964, in cross country and track to keep fit for walking. (Road running for women in those days was unknown!)

Judy Farr retired from race walking in 1981 after competing in the World Veterans Championships in New Zealand, due to a back injury.

As a member of Trowbridge and District Athletic Club, she set a British record for the number of consecutive Women Amateur Athletic Association titles. Between 1962 and 1970 she won the British 1½ mile/2,500km walk title nine times; she took ten titles in all, as she also won in 1960 as well. Judy Farr still lives in Trowbridge.

Janet Anderson – Politician

Janet Anderson is the daughter of the late Tom Anderson, Labour Party agent, and late Ethel née Pearson. She was born on 6 December 1949. When her father was Labour Party agent in Trowbridge in the early sixties, she went to Newtown Junior School, and then on to the Trowbridge High School. She then was educated at Kingsfield Comprehensive School, Bristol. Her further education began at the Polytechnic of Central London and later she gained a Diploma in Bi-lingual Business Studies from the University of Nantes in France. On 2 October 1972, she married Vincent Humphreys, a solicitor, the son of late William and Eleanor Humphreys. They now have two sons and a daughter: James, David and Kate.

Janet Anderson began her working career as a secretary on the newspapers *The Scotsman* and then the *Sunday Times*, from 1971 to 1974.

She joined the Labour Party in 1970 and her political career began in 1974, as personal assistant to the Rt Hon. Barbara Castle (later Baroness Castle of Blackburn) who was then Secretary of State for Social Services. She remained as her personal assistant when in 1979 Barbara Castle became a Member of the European Parliament, and Leader of the Labour Group within the European Parliament in 1979.

In 1981, Janet Anderson then became personal assistant to Jack Straw MP, who was at that time Shadow Treasury and Local Government Spokesman.

She stayed in this post for six years. In 1987 she became Campaigns Officer for the Parliamentary Labour Party, and then in 1989 was appointed as Co-ordinator of the Labour Party's 'Industry 2000' Campaign, headed by Gordon Brown.

1990 saw her working as the Northern Regional Organiser on the Shopping Hours Reform Council.

In 1987, she had contested the Rossendale and Darwen Constituency as a parliamentary candidate, but without success. However, she persevered and in the next general election, on 9 April 1992, she won the parliamentary seat from David Trippier MP. She became the first woman MP to represent the constituency, and was also the first Labour MP for Darwen.

She began her parliamentary career almost immediately as Parliamentary Private Secretary from 1992 to 1993 to Margaret Beckett MP, who was then Deputy Leader of the Labour Party. During this period she was also Parliamentary Labour Party Representative. The following year she served on the House of Commons Commission.

In 1995 to 1996 she was an Opposition Whip, responsible for ensuring that the Labour Party MPs voted on key issues, and the following year was appointed the Shadow Minister for Women.

Following the general election of 1997, when she retained her parliamentary seat with a majority of 10,949, Janet Anderson was appointed Vice-Chamberlain of Her Majesty's Household, an official title of a Government Whip.

She entered the government in 1998, being appointed Parliamentary Under-Secretary of State, in the Department for Culture, Media and Sport, as the Minister for Tourism, Film and Broadcasting.

Janet was re-elected in 1997, 2001 and 2005, but lost her seat in 2010.

During her parliamentary career she was a member of the Select Committees for Home Affairs from 1994–95, and Accommodation and Works 1997–98.

Within the Labour Party she was Vice Chair of the Labour Campaign for Electoral Reform and a Steering Committee Member of the Labour Women's Network. She was Secretary of the Tribune Group from 1993–96.

Among her other interests was as a member of the Parliamentary Panel, Royal College of Nursing from 1992–97. She was the Hon. Adviser to Emily's List UK.

Janet Anderson was also Vice-President of the Association of District Councils, and a Fellow of the Royal Society for the Arts.

Her special political interests include the footwear and textile industries, women's issues, health, constitution and constitutional issues, employment rights and protection, home affairs, culture, media and sport.

Among her recreations she includes playing the piano, and listening to opera.

Ken Rogers – Local Historian, Author and Archivist

Ken Rogers has had a huge influence on the way that Trowbridge is perceived and understood. His background as an archivist enabled him to discover and research key documents like the 1200 Trowbridge Market Charter, one of the earliest such charters in the country.

The author of the new *Buildings of Wiltshire* book, Julian Orbach, attributes to Ken Rogers the fact that the authoritative Wiltshire book, originally written by Sir Nikolaus Pevsner in the 1960s, included many more industrial buildings than the equivalent Somerset version. Ken Rogers went around Trowbridge with Pevsner in the 1960s and again with Julian Orbach in 2016. His work on the local woollen industry has been instrumental in the recognition that the woollen industry buildings in the town represent an 'outdoor museum of national importance.'

Ken was born in Dursley Road, Trowbridge in 1930. He attended Trinity Infants 1934–38, Trinity Junior Park Street then Newtown 1938–41, and Trowbridge Boys' High School 1941–49. Owing to the excellence of the teaching in maths and science, he, like most other boys there, took these subjects at Higher level, and actually began an engineering degree at Bristol. Finding, almost by accident, that it was possible to have a career as an archivist (then almost a new idea), he saw that it would suit his growing interest in history much better. National Service in the army provided an opportunity to change (the army actually paid for a correspondence course!) and he was able to return to Bristol in 1953, and took a first in History in 1956. The necessary archive training at University College, London, followed in 1956–57.

Ken's first job was as assistant archivist in the Cornwall Record Office at Truro, 1957–59. Then a vacancy arose as assistant editor of the Victoria County History of Wiltshire – to be actually paid to research local history in one's native county was too tempting! Unluckily, the account of Trowbridge had already appeared in Volume vii, but most of his period with the VCH was devoted to Volume viii, for which he wrote the sections on several adjoining parishes – North Bradley, Steeple Ashton and Keevil among them, as well as Warminster and surrounding area.

In 1964, however, a chance arose to return permanently to an archive career proper as Assistant County Archivist of Wiltshire. Ken remained at the Wiltshire Record Office for the rest of his working life, succeeding as County Archivist in 1981, and retiring in 1990.

His main interests have been two – the history of Trowbridge and the history of the local woollen industry. On the first he wrote *The Book of Trowbridge* in 1984 and *Medieval Trowbridge* in 2016, on the second *Wiltshire and Somerset Woollen Mills* in 1976 and *Warp and Weft* in 1986, as well as numerous articles and pamphlets on both subjects. He and his wife Helen (also a historian, formerly a librarian at the Institute of Historical Research) have both been deeply involved in all aspects of local history in the area, especially the development of Trowbridge Museum.

Ken Rogers' books include:

The Newcomen Engine in the West of England, 1976; *Wiltshire and Somerset Woollen Mills*, 1976; *Trowbridge in Pictures 1812–1914* (with M.J. Lansdown and M. Marshman), 1979; *The Book of Trowbridge*, 1984; *Warp and Weft, the Wiltshire and Somerset Woollen Industry*, 1986; *Trowbridge History and Guide*, 1994; *Trowbridge, Archive Photograph Series* (with M. Marshman), 1998; *Medieval Trowbridge*, 2016.

Also numerous Friends of Trowbridge Museum Series (Yellow Books) including *Clothiers' Workshops in Trowbridge*, *Power in the Trowbridge Woollen Industry*, *Woollen Industry Processes I – The Domestic Industry*, *Woollen Industry Processes II – The Factory Industry* and *The History of Roads in and around Trowbridge and the Traffic on them to about 1870*.

Trevor Porter – Newspaper Photographer

Trevor Porter lived just four doors away from the school, at number 90 Newtown. He fondly remembers Mrs Moody, one of his teachers, who has followed his career via the stories and pictures in the *Wiltshire Times*. Trevor says she helped lay the foundations of his education.

Trevor became a *Wiltshire Times* freelance photographer. Trevor was given his first camera at the age of twelve by his grandmother. However, it was to be the photographs he took when taking part in the sport of rallying that got him hooked. He later recalled in a *Wiltshire Times* interview that through this he had 'a picture on every national's front page and you can't help but get a buzz when that happens'.

Trevor has taken photos for the *Wiltshire Times* since 1980 and worked for the company full-time from 1999, now freelance, becoming very well-known across Wiltshire, and especially in his hometown of Trowbridge.

He was to make the headlines himself when he scooped an international award as an unsung hero. In 2012, he travelled to the headquarters of Gannett, the parent company of the *Wiltshire Times* owners, Newsquest, in Virginia in the United States. He was the only British journalist from Newsquest to be in the frame for an award.

As the *Wiltshire Times* article reported: 'Mr Porter was nominated by *Wiltshire Times* editor Gary Lawrence. He commended him for his perseverance in getting the best pictures, citing the time he hid for six hours in a building in Lacock to snap the filming of *Harry Potter*, an image craved by the world's media.

'Mr Lawrence said: "It is not just his photography that we rely on. He has got that ethic that if something needs doing, he'll do it." He was "commended for pulling out all the stops to get the best pictures and stories."'

Trevor recalled that one of his most memorable photos, capturing the story of a twelve-year-old boy in Sierra Leone, who had his leg amputated in the conflict.

Trevor later said, in an interview in the *Wiltshire Times*, 'That meant a lot to me. The lad had lost his parents and a mine went off and they had to cut his leg off. It left me very tearful. I'd love to go back one day and see what he is doing now.'

'When you get up in the morning, you just don't know what the day is going to throw at you. I have been very lucky in my time.'

Trevor said he 'takes inspiration in his job from his father, John Porter, who once told him: "If you're going to do a job, do it properly."

'He gave me the inspiration and I've always stuck to that. You only get out of a job what you put into it.'Comments on the story about the award in the *Wiltshire Times* pay tribute to his work with Emergency Services – 'being discreet and allowing others to do their work unhindered and without the worry of what he was going to publish'. Another said, 'after being called out in the most unsociable hours Trevor could be found in the office at 7am downloading the images of the night before ready for the editor's consideration … his commitment to "getting the shot" is admirable.'

Trevor was at the Centenary celebration of Newtown School and caught up with a former school contemporary, MP and minister Janet Anderson. He used his photographic skills to record the Centenary of a school he had attended decades earlier.

Those recorded above are, to some degree, a sample of the former pupils who have carved out successful careers in later life. They are obviously not alone. A few have had a significant impact on the town.

Councillor Bob Brice has been an important local figure in both the town and West Wiltshire as a leader of both West Wiltshire District and Trowbridge Town Councils. His commitment, knowledge and experience have been major assets to the town.

Jennifer Polledri, née Morphew, became Chairman of the Trowbridge & District Chamber of Commerce in the 1990s and subsequently President of the Chamber. In this role she was Chair of Trowbridge in Bloom. In 2009, with the revival of Trowbridge in Bloom, Jennifer again became chair and has made a major contribution to the life of the town. All the various cultural offshoots of Trowbridge in Bloom have generated pride and a sense of accomplishment in the town. Her commitment to young people through public speaking and story writing competitions, as well as previously a young business initiative, has done much to enrich and enhance our town.

There are obviously other former Newtownians who have contributed significantly to the town, and there will undoubtedly be others who will do so in the future.

TEACHING STAFF OF THE NEWTOWN/TRINITY SCHOOLS

The lists below attempt to include all the teaching staff who taught at all the Newtown/Trinity Schools for any length of time. Supply teachers, student teachers and pupil teachers have not been included.

Many of the staff taught at more than one school, as the administrative structures were changed. Elsie Blanchard was head of three of the schools – Trinity Girls, Holy Trinity Infants and Trinity Infants – for example.

The original Newtown Mixed and Infants Schools became just Newtown Mixed School, with the Infant Department joining with Holy Trinity to create Trinity Infant School. Newtown Mixed School, which was all-age at that point, was then divided once again, with the older children staying in the Newtown Building, and the Juniors joining with Trinity Juniors to create Trinity County Junior School in the Park Street Building. When Newtown Senior Boys School, as it briefly became, vacated the Newtown buildings and moved to the Galley Farm site to join with the Adcroft Schools to create Nelson Haden Schools, Trinity Junior became Newtown Junior, subsequently reopening the Park Street building for some years. Finally, and most recently, Newtown Junior and Trinity Infants joined to create Newtown Community Primary School 1993.

Teaching Staff of the Newtown British School / Newtown Senior School 1898–1940

Mr William Hodgson	1898–1931	Miss V. Ruth Pickett	1913–1933
(Head Teacher)		Mr. H. Leonard Scott	1913–1915
Miss Ada M. Chandler	1898–1906		1917–1925
Miss Rosa E. Hayward	1899–1912	Mr. P.W. Harris	1914–1916
Miss Edith Rose	1901–1913		1919
Mr Walter C. Deacon	1902–1907	Mr Nelson Welchman	1914
(Died in Post)			1919–1920
Mr J.J. Henley	1902–1903	Miss Elsie Holland	1915–1931
Mr Harold C. Croft	1904–1913	Miss Gladys L. Smith	1916–1919
Miss Sarah M. Sawtell	1906–1916	Mr B.H. Taylor	1916
Mr Ed H. Shield	1908–1914	Miss F. Sullivan	1916–1919
Miss S.A. Giddings	1913–1920	(Supply Cover for Mr Welchman)	

Miss L.R. Batchelor	1920–1922	Mr Charles F. Georges	1926
Miss G.E. (Nellie) Nurding	1920–1924	Miss E.E.E. Archbold	1927–1930
Miss Marion M. Richmond	1920–1924	Mr E.J.M. Fenton	1927–1934
Miss Edith M. Cox	1921–1940	Miss Winifred M. Harper	1927–1929
Miss Julia A. Stone	1922–1924	Mr Alfred D. Padfield	1928–1938
Mr Esiah Jones	1923–1924	**Mr Ernest Hughes**	1929–1940
Mr Fred R.M. Folkes	1924–1928	(Head Teacher)	
Mr David B.W. Jenkins	1924–1926	Miss C.M. Perrett	1929–1940
Miss C.E. Berrett	1925–1927	(Married 1937 Mrs C.M. Richards)	
Mr Louis A. Fletcher	1925–1926	Miss R.M. Young	1930–1931
Mr J.A. Bond	1926–1927	Mrs J. Bailey	1931–1940

On 31 August 1931, Newtown Mixed School became Newtown Senior School.

Mr William Rees	1931–1940	Mr Ernest Brown	1937–1940
Miss Alma G. Cox	1933–1936	Mr B.E.J. Waters	1938–1940
Mr T.J. Jones	1933–1935		

On 31 May 1940, Newtown became Newtown Senior Boys School. Adcroft became the girls' senior school.

Mr Ernest Hughes remained as head teacher of the Newtown School. The teaching staff at this point were Messrs Albert E. Angell, William Rees, C. Watts, W.G. Wakefield, B.E.J Waters, T. Blacka and Mr Taylor. On that date the girls moved to Adcroft Girls School and met at Trinity Church Hall and Bethesda Sunday School. The former Newtown Senior staff employed were Miss Edith G. Cox, Mrs C.M. Richards, Mrs J. Bailey.

In September 1940, Nelson Haden Secondary Schools opened on the Galley Farm site. Mr Ernest Hughes became head of Nelson Haden Boys School, and Miss V. Ruth Pickett, head of the Adcroft Girls School and formerly a member of Newtown Senior School staff, became head of Nelson Haden Girls School. Mr Albert (Skip) Angell was appointed temporary head of Nelson Haden Boys School during the transitional period.

Holy Trinity Girls School

The school began in 1836 but the school logbooks in the Wiltshire and Swindon Record Office only go back to 1899. However, anecdotal evidence gives a Miss Hill as head teacher in the 1880s.

Miss Hill	1880s	Miss Rose A. Simpkins	1908–1909
(Head Teacher)		Miss Gladys L. Smith	1909–1914
Miss Sarah J. Banwell	1899–1902	Miss Maude E. Webb	1914–1915
(Head Teacher)		**Miss Elsie E. Blanchard**	1915–1922
Miss Emily Randall	1899–1901	(Head Teacher)	
Miss Emma L. Wareham	1899–1913	Miss Margaret F. Mattock	1914–1918
(Certified from 1906)		(Became Mrs M.F. Cox)	1920–1922
Miss Sarah J. Vockings	1901–1908	Miss Mildred Culverhouse	1915–1917?
Miss Kate A. Wells	1902–1915	Miss May Randall	1917–1920
(Head Teacher)		(Became Mrs M. Inglis 1919)	
Miss C.E.M Heathcote	1905–1905	Miss Laura M. Smith	1917–1920
Miss Kate E. Watts	1906–1917	Miss Dorothy E. Giles	1918–1922
(Became Mrs K.E. Hayward –		Miss Winifred Harper	1920–1921
Taught in Trinity and Newtown			
Junior Schools 1932–1949)			

The decision by the church authorities to rationalise the church schooling in the town meant that, from 1923, girls from Holy Trinity Girls' School in Stallard Street were to go to Parochial Girls' School. The departure of the headmistress, Miss Elsie Blanchard, to become head of Trinity Infants in 1922, and the fact that the school was to be closed meant a succession of teachers were placed in charge of the school for very short periods of time, sometimes a matter of days during the last few months of its existence.

Teaching Staff of the Trinity Boys School/Trinity County Junior School/Newtown County Junior School.

These schools followed on from one another and some staff move on from one school to the other.

Trowbridge Trinity Boys School

Mr Henry (Harry) Moore	1873–1906	Mr William Borloae	1880–1882
(Head Teacher)		Mr John F. Gardiner	1882–1924
Mr N.J. Bigwood	1879–1880	Mr Harry Gerrish	1889–1889

Mr Walter J. Hail	1893–1894	Miss Ethel S. Balchelor	1916–1919
Mr George W. Naish	1894–1895	Mr Frank Musselwhite	1917–1919
Mr Percy S. Laslett	1895–1896	Mr Fred W. White	1919–1921
Mr Henry Dyer	1896–1897	Miss Nellie B. Gale	1920–1926
Mr Charles J. Spittle	1898–1899	Miss Ellen L. Angell	1922–1926
Mr Thomas G. Warren	1899–1901	Miss L.R. Batchelor	1923–1938
Mr Henry J. Stevens	1901–1914	(Later Mrs L.R. Moore 1934)	
	1917	Mr R.E. Noise	1923–1930
Mr Albert E. Knight	1905	Mr W.J. Marks	1924–1927
Mr Arthur C. Walter	1905–1908	**Mr William Dyke-Meek**	1926–1949
Mr C.V. Manley	1906–1913	(Head Teacher)	
(Head Teacher)		Mrs N.B. Beaven	1926–1944
Mr Harry C. Collings	1906–1916	Mr W.H. Long	1926–1927
(Killed in Action 1918)		Mrs Kate E. Hayward	1927–1949
Mr J.B. Clark	1908–1912	Mr Alexander Haywood	1927–1928
Robert A. Wesley	1913–1926		
(Head Teacher)			

1931 Trinity became Trinity Junior School

Miss Bessie W. Smith	1931–1933	Miss Marjorie E.A. White	1937–1943
(Later Mrs Rodway 1933)	1945–1966	Miss Emily G. Rogers	1939–1942
Mr Morgan R. Daniel	1930–1944	Miss Barbara M. Thomas	1939–1952
Miss Betty L. Joyce	1933–1938	Mrs Hilda Brabban	1940–1941

In 1940, Trinity County Junior School became Newtown County Junior School and moved into the Newtown Building.

Mrs M.E. Knott	1941–1943	Mr John R. Napthene	1948–1968
Miss Joan E. Beaven	1942–1948	Mr Cyril Sparks	1949–1960
Mrs V.E. Maslin	1942–1965	**Mr Ralph Warburton**	1949–1964
Mrs S. Milner	1943–1944	(Head Teacher)	
Mrs Dorothy V. Alpe	1944–1946	Miss J.H. Griffiths	1950–1951
Miss E.M. Learoyd	1944–1945	Miss Norah Bull	1952–1967
Miss Glennis D. Hillman	1945–1949	Mr H.J. Griffiths	1952–1953
Mrs M.H. Miller	1945–1963	Miss Myrtle Norman	1952–1959
Miss Gwendolen B. West	1945–1945	Miss J. Mary Balch	1953–1967
Mr John J. Boulding	1946–1952	(Became Mrs J.M. Stacey)	
Miss Avril C.E. Wickham	1947–1952	Mr Fred W.P. Stacey	1953–1960
Mr Frederick J.E. Ewings	1948–1960	Miss J.E. Wickham	1953–1954
Mrs Alice E.E. Moody	1948–1960	Mrs Mamie L. Perren	1954–1960

Miss Sheila M. Webb	1954–1956
(Became Mrs S.M. Courtney?)	
Miss Patricia A. Taylor	1955–1958
(Became Mrs P.A. Douglas)	
Miss Delia M. Denman	1956–1959
Miss Marian E. Gerrish*	1958–1962
Mrs C.Y. Cannell	1959–1960
Mrs J.M. Johnson	1959–1968
Mrs Betty Penny	1959–1975
Mrs Kath J. Foster	1960–1980
Mrs W.A. Hayes	1960–1964
Mr R. Paul Stacey	1960–1988
Miss Catherine Macsween	1963–1964
Miss C. Snelgrove	1964–
Mr John W. Hicks	1965–1982
(Head Teacher)	
Mr Mervyn J. Bush	1965–1991
Mrs Martineau	1965–1966
Miss Judith M. Amner	1966–1968
Mrs Vera Roberts	1966–1978
(Died in Post)	
Miss Myra G. Smith	1966–1993
(Later Mrs M.G. Green 1973)	
Mrs Gillian E. Adams	1967–1969
Mrs Barbara M. Lucas	1967–1993
Mrs Carol Miller	1967–1970
Mrs Judith Bolton	1968–1969
Mrs Frances Delaney	1968–1973
Mrs Julie E. Hall	1968–1969
Mr T.M. Milner	1968–1969
Mr Eddie P. Stephens	1968–1973
Mrs Betty F. Brant	1969–1981
Mrs V. Clark	1969–1970
Miss Sonia Davis	1969–1971
Mrs V.H. Holmes	1970
Mrs Barbara A. Bennett	1970–1972
Miss Audrey M. Clode	1971–1973
Mrs Celia Davies	1971–1989
Mrs Mary A. McDonald	1971–1972
Miss Christine Hart	1972–1974
Mr Keith Shipton	1972–1974
Mr Andy Milroy	1972–1993
Mrs M.A. Barnett	1973–1974
Mrs Ann Priest	1973–1978
Mrs Sheila Priest	1973–1974
Mrs Diane Burrell	1974
Mrs Margaret Gray	1974–1975
Miss Neta Hallsworth	1974–1978
Mrs M.E. Hill	1974
Mr Tony E. Smith	1974
Mrs Ann Williams	1974
	1978–1992
Miss Sarah Wood	1974–1978
(Became Mrs S. Lund)	
Miss Kathy M. Yeaman	1974–1980
(Became Mrs K.M. Torrance)	
Mrs Jill Burge	1975–1977
Mrs Margo Ward	1978–1982
Mrs Elizabeth Hincks	1979–1988
Mrs Lorna Letters	1979–1993
Miss Lin Moore	1979–1988
(Later Mrs L. Harris)	
Mrs Monica Ridgway	1979–1980
Miss Lois Francis	1981–1985
Mr Tim Hill	1982–1984
(Head Teacher)	
Mr Richard Craft	1985–1993
(Head Teacher)	
Miss Josephine Cutting	1985–1993
Mrs Bella Osbourne	1985–1986
Miss Hayley Butt	1986–1987
Mrs Stella Leeder	1986
Miss Kerrie Rogers	1987–1991
(Later Mrs K. McNeill)	
Mr Stan Emery	1988–1993
Miss Sarah Nell	1988–1991
Mrs Allyson Sourey	1988–1993
Mrs Liz Surowiec	1989–1993

| Mrs Alison Brown | 1991–1992 | Mr Chris Paul | 1991–1992 |
| Mrs Amanda King | 1991–1992 | Mrs Julie Park | 1991–1993 |

The Teaching Staff of the Newtown/ Holy Trinity and Trinity Infant Schools 1898–1993

Newtown

Miss Ada M. Chandler	1898–1900	Miss F.R. Chevrill	1909–1917
Miss Cooper	1898–1900?	Miss Elsie W. Payne	1913–1921
Miss Letitia Rogers	1900–1916	Miss B. Hudd	1916–1921
(Became Mrs L. Pearce 1915)		Miss Winifred L. Cole	1917–1919
Miss Amy Grant	1901–1904	(Became Mrs W.L. York)	1921–1945
Miss Margaret Hartley	1902–1931	Miss Una Burnett	1919–1928
(Head Teacher)		Miss Julia A. Stone	1921–1922
Miss Amy Cox	1905–1908	Miss Flora Keates	1925–1928
Miss Pildrem	1905–1913		1928–1933

Holy Trinity

Miss L.H. Gibson	1896–1901	Miss A.E. Brewer	1907–1911
(Head Teacher)		Miss Dorothy Puckeridge 1907	
Miss R.E. Dobson	1896–1901	Miss F. Noke	1909–
Miss Ellen Holland	1901–1902	Miss Emily G. Pike	1913–1917
(Head Teacher)		Miss Hart	1917–1918
Miss Grace Baldwin	1901–1903	Miss M.H. Love	1918–1922
Miss Mary A. Weller	1902–1922	Miss D. Smith	1918–1922?
(Head Teacher)		**Miss Elsie Blanchard**	1923–1947
Miss Annie Slugg	1904–1909	(Head Teacher)	
Miss Lily M. Say	1905–1951	Miss Kathleen Cottle	1925–1935

In 1928, Trinity Infants was built and staff from Holy Trinity and Newtown Infants moved over to the new Trinity Infant School.

Miss Stella E.M. Cook	1933–1947	Miss Muriel I. Davies	1938–1949
Miss Eleanor Dangerfield	1935–1939	(Became Mrs M.I. Jones 1942)	
Miss Doreen M. Howard	1935–1952	Miss J. M. Bullock	1939–1942
Miss Hilda M. Paul	1935–1938	(Became Mrs J.M. Priest 1941)	
Miss Evelyn M. Usher	1935–1937	Miss Ivy I. Manners	1939–1942
Miss Edith E. Thomson	1937–1940	(Became Mrs I.I. Eckles 1941)	

Miss Alma E. Comley   1942–1948
(Became Mrs A.E. Jones)

Mrs Matthias   1942–1945

Miss Ailsa Bingham   1945–1946
(Became Mrs A. Busse 1945)

Mrs G. Jones   1945–1946
(Formerly Mrs Humphreys)

Miss Barbara E.M. Pyart 1946–1948

Miss Avril C.E. Wickham 1946–1947

Miss Edna M. Hall   1947–1955
(Head Teacher)

Miss Celia Manley   1947–1948

Miss Josephine M. Booth 1948–1952
(Became Mrs J.M. Perrott)

Miss Marion J. Gooch   1948–1949

Miss Marion J. Harvey   1948–1959

Mrs Winifred Sleightholme 1949–1968
(Head Teacher 1959–1968)

Miss Marigold De Courcy-Ireland
                         1949–1951

Miss Sheila M. Smith   1949–1951

Miss Rita M. Creed   1951–1954

Miss Sylvia M. Green   1951–1954?
(Became Mrs S.M. Plenty)

Miss Ann Knight   1951–1956?
(Became Mrs A. Housden)

Mrs Cynthia Colin   1952–1958

Miss Dorothy J. Williams 1952–1954

Miss J.C.B. Davis   1953–1962

Miss B. Leech   1954–1961?
(Became Mrs B. Ling?)

Mrs P.A. Randall   1955

Mrs M.D. Hamling   1956–1957

Mrs M.I. Jones   1956–1957

Miss Olive Richardson 1956–1959
(Head Teacher)

Miss D.J. Clack   1957–1960

Mrs J. Shaw   1957–1960

Miss Marion E. Gerrish* 1958–1962

Mrs P.M. Bishop   1959–1960

Miss M.S. Smith   1959–1960

Miss June A. Plumb   1960–1982
(Became Mrs J.A. Harrison)

Mrs Georgina M. Slade   1960–1964
                         1967–1982

Miss Margaret Payne   1961

Miss N. Simpson   1961

Miss Meta O. Carter   1962–1967

Mrs J.D. Venton   1962–1964

Miss J.M. Betteridge   1964

Miss Marion C. Hanks   1964–1980

Mrs S. Perkins   1964–1970
(Died in Post)

Mrs M. Rowlands   1964–1967

Mrs Gillian E. Adams   1965–1967

Mrs Susan Prior   1966–1986

Mrs Margaret Strawbridge 1966–1968

Mrs Maureen Elsom   1967–1973

Mrs Kotlarz   1967–1968

Mrs J. Metcalf   1967–1969

Mrs E. Joan Doel   1968–1984
(Head Teacher)

Mrs Corinne Gregory   1968–

Miss Priest   1969–

Miss Ann Liddiard   1970–1974
(Became Mrs A. Jarrett)

Miss Patricia Christison 1971

Mrs Shirley Katzmarck   1971

Mrs Terese Mustoffi   1971–1974

Barbara Faragher   1972–1974

Mrs Wendy Jones   1972–1992

Mrs Cath Senior   1972–1988

Maureen Balfour   1974–

Mrs Joyce Ballenger   1974–1988?

Sue Crawley   1974–

Mrs Anthea Courage   1974–1997

*Note Marion Gerrish taught at both Trinity Infants and Newtown Junior Schools during this period – probably a joint appointment.

Jane Scowcroft	1974–	Jean Jane	1984–1985?
Mrs Sue Selwyn–Smith	1974–1993	Chris Heywood	Left 1988
Mrs Doreen Sykes	1974–1977?	Mrs Claire Gunstone	1985–1993
Mary Harnot	1976–1976	Mrs Anne Carter	1986–1993
Miss Myra Grant	1977–1984	Mrs Jean Sellars	1986–1992
Mrs Julie Venner	1978–	Mrs Jennifer Williams	1986–1993
Mrs Veronica Parker	1984–1991	Mrs Liz Steele	1987–1993
(Head Teacher)		Miss Angela Bennett	1988–
Rosemary Geeke	1984–1986	Miss Jo Hooson	1988–1993
Ann Harvey	1984–1987?		
(Died in Post)			

Newtown County Primary School 1993

Mr Richard Craft	1993–2000	Mrs Chris Watson	1996
(Head Teacher)		Mrs Sarah Pender	1997–1998
Mrs Anne Carter	1993–2004	Mrs Angie Seaman	1997–2000
(Deputy Head 1993–1994)		(Became Mrs A. Pearce)	
Miss Jo Cutting	1993–1996	Mrs Carol Hill	1998–2016
Mrs Claire Gunstone	1993–2007	Mrs Jeanne Hudd	1998–2000?
Mrs Jo Hooson	1993–1994	Ms Nikki Weir	1999–2000?
Mrs Barbara Lucas	1993–2003	Miss Sarah Fulker	2000–2005/6?
Mr Andy Milroy	1993–2003	Miss Liz Morton	2000–2005/6?
Mrs Sue Selwyn-Smith	1993–2003	Mrs Jan Stallard	2000–2001
Mrs Liz Steele	1993–1998		
Mrs Liz Surowiec	1993–2002?	**Subsequent Headteachers**	
Mrs Jennifer Williams	1993–2005	Mrs Sue Ivermee	2000–2004
Miss Laurie Johnson	1994	Mrs Marian Bartlet	2004–2009
Mr Mike Tozer	1994–2007	Mr Tom Hill	2010–2011
Miss Sue Harding	1996–1997	Mrs Mary Hiscocks	2012–2015
Mrs Caroline Hider	1996–2000	Mr Chris Marshall	2015–
Miss Jenny Mcdonald	1996–1999		

AFTERWORD

This book is a series of snapshots, recording the story of a school over a hundred years; describing the interaction between community, teachers, parents and of course, children.

Every school is distinctive, perhaps I am biased, but to me Newtown seems particularly unique. I hope you agree.

#0024 - 100118 - C0 - 234/156/12 - PB - 9781780915685